AMBUSHED

AMBUSHED

Judith Ward

VERMILION
London

First published 1993

1 3 5 7 9 10 8 6 4 2

Judith Ward has asserted her right under the Copyright, Designs and Patents Act, 1988 to be identified as the author of this work

First published in the United Kingdom in 1993 by Vermilion
an imprint of Ebury Press
Random House UK Ltd, 20 Vauxhall Bridge Road
London SW1V 2SA

Random House Australia (Pty) Limited
20 Alfred Street, Milsons Point, Sydney
New South Wales 1061. Australia

Random House New Zealand Limited
18 Poland Road, Glenfield
Auckland 10, New Zealand

Random House South Africa (Pty) Limited
PO Box 337, Bergvlei, South Africa

Random House UK Limited Reg. No. 9540009

A CIP catalogue record for this book
is available from the British Library

ISBN 0 09 1778204

Printed in England by Clays Ltd, St Ives plc
Typeset in Palatino by SX Composing Ltd, Rayleigh, Essex

I dedicate this book to my Mum and Dad,
Michael Farrell,
SR Sarah Clarke,
Paul May
and
Gareth Peirce

Acknowledgements

With grateful thanks to Susan Hill for her invaluable help and advice. To Rowena Webb, my publisher, for her patience. To all the inmates and staff who supported me over the years, especially Lorna, Martina and Ella. Above all a special thanks to that walking calendar of a copy editor Beth Humphries.

Contents

H Wing, HMP Durham, September 1975   1

1   Liverpool, 14 February 1974   5
2   Memories 1949-66   10
3   Ireland 1966-70   18
4   Army, Ireland, Arrest 1970-74   25
5   Remand and Trial, 1974   34
6   Durham 1974-76   42
7   Durham 1976-84   57
8   Durham 1984-86   75
9   Cookham Wood, Holloway, Durham, 1987-90   106
10   Holloway 1990   135
11   Appeal, 1991-92   149
12   Freedom   168

Index   178

H Wing, HMP Durham, September 1975

I awoke under a pale yellow glow. Faces stared down on me. Hands on my arms, soothing touches, damp and cool. I raised my head, saw tiny streams of blood running down on to a bright yellow bedspread.

'Lie still,' a voice commanded, 'we have to bandage your arms.' I lay back. No panic, I thought, not caring, floating along with the black velvet quiet of the night.

'Will she need stitches?' I recognised the Governor's voice.

'No sir, they're not bad. She'll be scarred, though.' A male voice, probably one of the nursing officers.

'Do you think she's in shock? She looks a bit pale.' A young female voice, slightly anxious, trying to seem unconcerned.

'After the night's performances, I'm sure I'd be a bit shocked too.'

Then I remembered what I'd wanted to forget. The 'night's performances' began just after tea. It was another boring night on H Wing, women watching TV, doing their washing or just talking to each other. Although it was quiet there was tension in the air, as if something were about to happen. This feeling often pervaded the prison atmosphere, where inmates were so bored I often thought they willed something, anything, to happen to break the mind-numbing routine. I had been sitting with my friend in her cell, chatting about nothing. I left to go to the loo and passed the shower room, just as an inmate, June, was entering.

'About time you had a wash,' I joked as she entered.

She smiled as she pushed open the door and turned to go in. She stopped and screamed loudly, then ran past me, a look of horror on her face. 'What's wrong?' I asked. Receiving no answer, I entered the shower room and couldn't believe my eyes. It looked as if someone had been murdered: there was blood on the walls, on the shower curtain, mingling with the water as it trickled down the plug-hole, past the unconscious, naked body of a woman. I jumped into the shower and turned off the water. Helen, another inmate, came in, alerted by June's scream and together we pulled the woman out of the shower on to the bench at the far wall. It was Monica, a drug addict serving four years; she was deadly white. We covered her with a towel, noting the gash halfway up her left arm, the skin slashed through to the artery, which pulsated slowly. Feeling sick, we made way for the officers and the nursing sister who had just arrived. As we stumbled out, other women called to us: 'What's happening Jude?', 'What's all the panic then – someone topped themselves?'

An officer came out of the shower: 'Just go to your cells, please, nothing to panic about' – the standard phrase and procedure used by the staff when an incident occurred. They usually locked everyone in, in an effort to stop panic spreading, which was quite illogical because the inmates then had no idea what was happening and their imaginations went wild, creating more panic than if they saw what was happening. If it had been daytime, we would have been locked in, but with only an evening staff of three officers and one nursing sister, nobody moved. It was 'an event' and no one wanted to miss it: every ghoulish minute would be recorded and stored, ready to relate in the future boring days to come. That night was to have more than one 'event'.

Earlier that evening, Janet had asked to be locked in her cell. She didn't want to 'associate' because she'd had bad news in a letter. Association is that period of time which inmates spend out of their cells, in company with each other. During the evenings, you could ask to be locked in your cell, which women sometimes did, although it wasn't usual. One of the officers thought she might start to worry with all the noise going on and had decided to go and have a few words with her. But Janet had heard the news anyway, and feeling down herself, decided that tonight was the night to end it all. She grabbed a mug, smashed it and used it to 'cut up'. By the time the officer got to her she'd done quite a good job. 'Cutting up' – inflicting wounds on oneself – is common in women's prisons. Male inmates tend to fight and be aggressive; women can also be aggressive, although the majority tend to withdraw into themselves and often relieve their depression, anger or guilt by inflicting pain on themselves. It could almost be said to be an urge to self-destruct, which in many cases it was, but for others it was the relieving of tension or other emotions, a cry for help, which is always present in any prison but generally goes unheeded. The other officers and the nurse ran round to Janet's cell and Helen and I were left to look after Monica, who was still unconscious. Mary, who occupied the cell next to the shower room, came out to ask, 'What's all the bleeding racket about?' We told her, not knowing that half an hour earlier she had downed a week's medicine, which she had secretly saved in her cell. When she heard what was happening, she went off her head. Screaming and yelling, she tried to climb out of her cell window. It's impossible for a cockroach to get through three sets of bars and a grille, so Mary had no chance; still, she gave it a go. It took six of us to hold her on the bed for twenty minutes until she calmed down. The wing was now in uproar. Three officers and one nurse were trying to calm down those who had become hysterical, phone for assistance and make sure no one bled to death.

I couldn't take in what the hell was going on. Sometimes you just act by instinct. I didn't panic or scream, or even wonder why it was all happening. I was just caught up in it all, struggling to make some kind of sense, some logic, where the rules of logic don't apply. Half an hour later, calm was restored, everyone was locked in. That's the way the system deals with 'events' like these – they lock everyone up, including the injured, or dope them with whatever type and strength of drug is going to have the greatest effect. You may refuse to take any drugs, but on a night such as this, few did. That night we got both: we were locked up and then the nursing sister came round to offer medicine. Maybe I should have taken some that night, I don't know.

All I know is, I was afraid, depressed, frustrated, angry and filled with sadness. How I hated this place, hated the 'screws', the inmates; most of all I hated myself. What kind of idiot was I, thinking that things would change, that some day I would be free of this life, this locking in, this depressing, claustrophobic box, filled with sad, frustrated despairing people. Why should I put up with it? Wouldn't it be better to end it all? With the alternative being nothing but sameness for years to come, the idea was attractive. I searched around for something sharp, anything. I stared round the room and my eyes lit upon the records. I plucked one out of its sleeve, broke it and began to cut.

I awoke under a pale yellow glow. . .

1

Liverpool, 14 February 1974

I backed up further into the shop doorway to avoid the pelting rain. There would be no lovers' meeting this St Valentine's night, unless it was in front of the TV curled up with a cup of Horlicks, which is exactly where I wished I was at this particular moment. I had hitched a lift on a whim, a desire to move from a depressing couple of days in Cardiff and found myself, on an equally depressing day, in Liverpool. It was 14 February, 1974, a Thursday, in the early hours of the morning and I was holed up in the doorway, nowhere to sleep, with no belongings, except for the clothes I wore, no money to buy food; a bum, a bag lady without the bags. For the last few weeks I had been wandering round London, sleeping rough, sometimes not sleeping at all, perpetually hungry, wondering what the hell I was doing but at the same time not caring, stuck in a void. I wanted to do something, anything, but I lacked the energy, physically or mentally, to pull myself together and sort myself out. I could have gone to my parents' house and started all over again, but then I would have to admit to myself and them that I was unable to cope. Washed out, I had 'celebrated' my twenty-fifth birthday four days ago and I felt a total failure.

I looked up and down the cold, dark street. There was no one around. I wanted to lie down and sleep, but it was too cold and damp. A large, dark blue van appeared round the corner and pulled up about 200 hundred yards away. I heard men's voices and drew back into the doorway: a van with more than one man in, when you were alone in the early hours, spelt trouble. I was debating whether to try and move on when the van moved down the road towards me. As it pulled alongside I felt a great sense of relief as I saw the word POLICE in bold, white letters on the side. There were three policemen inside. One of them jumped out as the van stopped.

'What are you doing here at this time of the morning, Miss?'

I was in a quandary now: if I said I had no money and no-where to go, I could be arrested for vagrancy.

'I'm just waiting for a friend to pick me up,' I answered, trying to appear confident. 'I've just phoned her and she's on her way in now.'

'At this hour?' He didn't seem convinced. 'How did you get here, and where are you going to?'

Nosey sod, I thought. 'I've come from London and eventually I hope to get back to Ireland, when I get some money.'

'Ireland, eh?' He stuck out his hand. 'Have you any identification on you?'

I gave him my driving licence. He examined it and took it across to the other two men in the van. After a few minutes he returned.

'This is a Northern Ireland licence. Are you from the North?' he asked as he held on to it.

'I usually live in the South, but I took the test in the North because you can get it quicker and I believe you can use this licence in England.' I was beginning to regret my earlier feeling of relief when they appeared.

He went back to his mates and then said, 'Would you mind coming to the station so we can check this licence?'

'Not at all,' I said. At least it would be warm. Little did I know how hot it was going to be! That relief I had felt earlier when I realised they were police was an irony that would stick with me for a long time to come.

The police station was warm and had a dampish aroma of wet coats. I was taken to an office at the back. They took the licence and left. I lit a cigarette and after a few minutes my eyes began to droop sleepily as the warmth overtook me. The door was abruptly opened and a policeman and woman entered. They didn't look particularly friendly. She stood near the door as he approached, driving licence in hand.

'This document is false!' Stern features, unsmiling mouth. 'The address on it is a factory, so where did you get it?'

I explained again that I had taken the test in Northern Ireland, but as I was living in the South at the time I didn't have an address in the North, so the driving instructor had given me this one.

'Do you mind if this policewoman searches you?' he asked, slightly mollified. I couldn't see what a driving licence had to do with a search, but I didn't object. We went off to the loo, where I took all my clothes off behind the toilet door and handed them to the policewoman. She searched them, seemed satisfied, I put them back on and we returned to the office. Left alone again, I settled down in the chair and began to nod off. The door opened and two men in plain clothes entered. They introduced themselves, but I can't remember their names. In fact, I don't remember much of the next five days.

All that remains is an overwhelming sense of tiredness, an exhaustion which sapped the will, a feeling of total isolation, a frightening hostility; they wanted answers to what seemed liked thousands of questions and I wanted, more than anything, just to sleep. Disjointed images appear in my mind – movements from one office to another, from one station to another, raised voices, angry faces. I know that at some stages my hands were tested to see whether I had handled nitroglycerine. And at some point they took away my clothes and gave me others, not mine, and horrible looking; I know that at some stage I confessed to planting a bomb and later refuted this confession. I don't know where I was or when these events took place. I had reached a point of no return, willing to say anything so that these people would go away, stop their eternal questions, so I could sleep, wash and feel human again.

It is interesting to note here that, although I had made a confession to planting the bomb, within two days the police were aware through their enquiries that I could not possibly have done so. Yet instead of sitting down and thinking about this, they just changed course and began to interrogate me on other bombing incidents, so eager were they to gain a confession.

People who have never come into contact with the police think that you have nothing to be afraid of if you're innocent, so why worry? It's not that simple. You have to prove you're innocent, you have to remember every detail of every day for the last few months. Where were you three weeks ago at 6 p.m. in the evening, and who were you with? Unless you're a walking diary, with a record of every minute of every day, there's no chance of remembering. I tried, but I knew I hadn't done anything like they were suggesting. First I was cocky and defiant then afraid and desperate. I asked for a solicitor when I realised they were serious, because it had to be a joke. Me, an insecure, immature, stupid snot-nosed kid from Stockport, a bum, involved in planting bombs?!

'Why do you need a solicitor if you've done nothing?' Why indeed! So instead of holding out against them I caved in, agreed with them. That was my undoing: I needed someone sane, logical to sort out this mess, someone I could talk to without being shouted at, someone I could get some sense out of. Maybe he or she could calm everyone down, break the chain of madness we were all caught up in, the entanglement of deceit and lies, truths and half-truths.

For five days and five nights everyone wanted answers. My mind was in chaos: in turn I was afraid and near to tears, then cocky and obstinate. Then I reached the point of no return, indifference. I was no longer thinking, just being, caught up in a whirlpool where only emotions existed. Nothing mattered any more, and finally I was left to lose myself in sleep. Travelling in a car on the road to Wakefield in the early hours of a Sunday morning, I fell into a deep sleep. On awakening I found myself in an even more complex situation. Here the police were soft-spoken and considerate and I had no defences left: I crumbled under their kindness. Again the questions and in a pathetic eagerness, generated by their subtlety, I answered. I have since learnt that the technique of using two different approaches – alternating the aggressive, loud-voiced, threatening copper with the soft-spoken, sympathetic, friendly one – is widely employed by the police to confuse the suspect and break down their defences.

It's very hard for me to try and assess now what really happened to me then. The passage of time and my mental state at the time give only fleeting impressions: sharp-looking policemen throwing accusatory glances and knife-edged words, which cut me into little pieces, kindly-faced policemen with offers of tea and cigarettes gently persuading me that it's best to 'tell all'. It all added to my confusion – even more so when they took me to the police canteen, bought me a lager and allowed me to watch TV! How was I to make any sense out of these contradictory events? One moment I'm the worst, most reviled creature living, the next I'm the guest of honour being offered free beer and sitting amongst twenty or so young policemen watching television. The programme was, ironically *Within These Walls*, a prison soap starring Googie Withers. I have been asked if I confessed in an effort to please. I haven't a clue. I was just an inert blob, being shunted from one place to another: feelings, emotions, logic and rationality had no meaning, my only purpose was to get away from these people. I escaped mentally by shutting down, distancing myself from them and any threat the near future could bring.

Being physically small, I was aware that I was an easy target for bullies: whether in playgrounds, police stations or prisons, slight physical stature makes one an easy candidate for aggression. In prison I learnt to defend myself, to pre-empt physical attacks by being lippy and creating an impression that I was some fearless little firebrand with whom it would be unwise to mess. It usually worked if I was picked on but in women's prisons there are relatively few bullies. Women's energies are usually much more preoccupied with worrying about what is happening to their homes and families, and they are generally much less prone to riots and violence than men. But it was years before I was able to stand up for myself well, defend myself cogently or realise what traps I was being led into. At the time of my arrest I was the proverbial lamb to the slaughter. I simply didn't have the ability to know where all those questions were leading, what constructions were being put on statements I made about my life in Ireland. Many of the people I had met held political views, some strong, some not, views that were aired freely in public. Believing in a united Ireland does not mean you support the IRA. There are Protestants who deplore the fact that jobs in places like the shipyard in Belfast are seldom given to Catholics; this doesn't mean they are about to change their church. Was it wrong to state my views as I honestly felt them? Was it such a crime?

2

Memories 1949–66

Memories of a green, daisy-filled meadow. A picnic, table-cloth laid under a huge oak tree. Dad snoring in the shade, Mum laying out the food, kids playing by the stream. Beakers, plates and bottles strewn around, Mum stands and calls to the kids to come and eat. Memories of a small, hot kitchen, Mum wiping floury hands on her apron, kids sitting at the table, drawing, reading, making models. All waiting for Dad so they can engage in a noisy family teatime. Family memories – not mine, unfortunately.

Compared to many people, I remember little about my childhood. A vague image of eating a round boiled 'lolly', which stuck in my throat, and Dad holding me upside down by the ankles to loosen it. Images of packing furniture to move house, which we seemed to do a few times before I was nine or ten. Most of the memories I have are painful so, perhaps subconsciously, I have wiped them out. More likely is the fact that these years never left much impression: mainly dull in routine, a generally uneventful and passive existence. Dominated by a volatile father, we were never demonstrative or affectionate to one another, a family in name only.

I was born in Stockport, Cheshire in 1949, third child and eldest daughter of Ethel and Terence Ward. I have two older brothers, Eric and Terence, a younger sister Elaine and younger again were the twins Anne and Peter. Like most families around us, we lived in a succession of tiny terraced houses, before moving to a three-bedroomed semi-detached house on a fairly new housing estate. By our standards it was quite modern and had a garden front and back, but I still shared the bed with Elaine and the twins, who were placed in the middle to stop them falling out. There was a dining-room too, which we rarely, if ever, used. Most meals were taken in the kitchen and few of them involved all of us sitting down together as a family unit.

My father created a lot of tension in the house. He had had a succession of jobs in the steel industry, but often lost them due to his drinking habits, which turned him into a vicious and spiteful man. He often came home drunk and would sometimes attack my mother. I was afraid of him and despised him. Even into my twenties I couldn't abide people who drank and wouldn't go into a pub, so strong were the memories of 'the old man', as we termed him. Eventually my mother divorced him and I, for one, was not sorry to see him go; his only legacy to me was a deep and abiding hatred of drunks and bullies. I saw him a couple of times after the divorce. My early memory is of a tall man, handsome in a brutish sort of way; I suppose all kids view their fathers as giants. He was, in fact, short, bald and fat the last time I saw him. He died many years later whilst I was in prison. I didn't mourn him.

When I was ten or eleven, my mother was expecting twins again and had to go into hospital early because of complications. I, as eldest girl, had to look after the others. I tried to keep house and kids clean and feed them with the bit of money I managed to drag out of the old man before he drank it all, but my efforts didn't impress my mum. One night she came from the hospital accompanied by two ambulancemen, worried about how we were coping. She was appalled by what she saw and had a terrible row with the old man, who'd just got back from the pub. He, as usual, started to get violent, the ambulancemen intervened, a fist fight broke out, the police were called. The result was that Mum was carted back off to hospital, the old man was carted off to the police station and we children were carted off to the kids' home. We were there for about three months; it wasn't too bad, I suppose. The worst thing was having to wear the uniform so all the other kids at school knew you were at the home. I was more worried about the twins who, being eight years younger than me, had been placed in an under-fives' home. As we'd never been separated before I wondered how they would react, although when we eventually got back together it didn't seem to have made any great impression on them.

We stayed at the home over Christmas and were allowed to visit Mum on Boxing Day. She seemed well, but of the twin babies she'd been expecting there was no sign. I thought perhaps they'd died. It wasn't until years later that I found out they'd been adopted. I have wondered since where they are and what they are doing: do they know they have three sisters and three brothers somewhere? Poor Mum, surely it must have been very difficult for her to have them adopted, but there is no way she could have looked after them. She already had four under the age of twelve to look after and with the divorce and the fact that she hadn't recovered properly from the Caesarian, which would mean months of lying in bed and no real money coming into the house, who could blame her? After Christmas we all went home, but Mum fell ill and had to go back into hospital and so we were off again, to a foster home this time. It was OK, but the 'Aunt' and 'Uncle' decided they had a real group of slaves under them. We were all given different 'chores' to do, after and before school. We thought it a bit much, but we did them anyway; the place was so boring, and we were only there for a few weeks until we returned home at Easter.

Mum's complications with her operation meant that a nurse used to call every day to make sure she was all right. Because of this, I didn't go to school for about nine or ten months. I stayed at home, cleaning, making the beds and 'cooking' endless tins of beans for the kids' meals. I still feel quite ambiguous about whether I enjoyed this time or not. I quite liked school, most of the classes anyway, but the idea of being allowed, officially, to stay off for so long was exciting too. Mum started to get well and began working. She had two or three cleaning jobs every week, at different houses, so I came home and got the tea ready, and when she came in all she had to do was eat it. She put in a lot of hours and we rarely saw her except at weekends. This wasn't unusual in our area. Many wives went out cleaning and the kids were left in the care of an elder child: the 'latch-key' kids they call us now, and great discussions revolve around the effects this had on us. Unfortunately one effect is that this way of living doesn't do much for family relationships; each member acts totally independently in such a way that the term 'family' means you're related only by name, with no sense of close-ness or belonging. However, faced with providing for a family and keeping them from being taken into care, there's not much many single parents can do.

I went back to school. I enjoyed geography, history, art and English, but hated sewing, cookery and maths and often 'knicked off' during these classes, usually going up to Man-chester and hanging around the city centre. I didn't have many friends at school, just a few who shared the same dis-like of classes. I was quiet, shy, immature and prone to sitting at home reading, usually adventure stories, autobiog-raphies and travel books, trying to imagine myself anywhere but where I was. My mother once told me of an incident when I was a small child that in some way shows just how shy I was. We had aunts and uncles, but they didn't figure much in our daily lives; some we visited maybe once or twice, others I've never met, and it was the same with grand-parents. One day my mother had to go out and couldn't take me with her, so she left me with my granny. When she left I was sitting on the stairs in the hallway and when she re-turned a couple of hours later I was still sitting there. I hadn't spoken to anyone and couldn't be cajoled into leaving the stairs. The episode left Granny with a guilty feeling that per-haps she'd done or said something wrong. As my mother told me, Granny was quite upset about it.

The years before I left school were dull. Quiet routines of Saturday shopping, dragging the twins along to get them out of Mum's way whilst she cleaned the house. The one phrase that really used to get to me was 'take the twins'. They were lovely-looking kids, blonde hair, blue eyes, I was quite proud of them really, but you don't need them dragging round after you everywhere you go. When I was shopping and they were grizzling in that whiney way kids can, I used to take a chocolate bar off the shop shelf and give it to them, with strict instructions: 'Eat it before we pay'! That was the extent of my criminal activities – except for the Great Milk Robbery!

A few friends from school decided they were going up to Lymme Park, an area of woods, fields and lake surrounding a large Elizabethan house. Lots of people used to go there in the summer, it was great for getting away from grey old housing estates. One summer Sunday morning we all met up to catch the train. We didn't have much money except for the fare. Pocket money was one of the things I never had a lot of. Well, we were walking up the road at around 8 a.m. It was quiet and warm and someone said we should have brought something to drink. We all agreed, but no one had any extra money. Then we saw the rows of milk bottles sitting on the steps, just asking to be taken, so we ran over and grabbed a bottle or two each. We legged it down the road, laughing hysterically and a little fearfully. Never having nicked anything of note before, we thought we were greatly daring and outrageous. When we got to the park we climbed up to the top of a hill: the view was fantastic, you could see right across Cheshire and Derbyshire. One of my friends, Sue, had sewn little bells on to the bottom of her trousers; they chimed merrily as we strolled along. Deer roamed free among the woods and fields of the park. We met a large herd as we came down from the hill. They were obviously entranced by the sound from the bells on Sue's trousers. As they followed us down, as first we thought it was a laugh, but as they neared us we got a bit frightened. Being 'townies' and not knowing whether they would attack or not, we began to run. So did they. Finally we jumped over a wall and collapsed in a giggling heap, with the deer staring over at us.

I had a few little adventures like this, pleasant and totally silly in remembrance, but it was a bit of a silly era. We wore those ridiculous bell-bottoms, or fixed cut-out triangle flares into the hems of our jeans if we couldn't afford the real thing. We loved the Beatles and the Stones, and I also loved Joan Baez and Bob Dylan: their songs had some sense to them and made a point about real issues. I don't know if this is where my social conscience began to grow, but the anger in some of the songs certainly struck a chord in me. By the time I left school at fifteen I was beginning to awaken to the fact that not everyone was equal in this world and that some people had a rough deal, because they were a different colour or held different ideas to others. I don't think I realised this consciously; it was more of a gut reaction when I heard songs like those of Joan Baez.

So, it was time for leaving – school and home. I'd already

decided that I wanted to get away from Stockport. Where to, I'd no idea, so what did I want? I wanted to work in the open, definitely not in a desk job, the thought of working nine to five every day just made me cringe. I wanted a job where something different happened now and again. For the last couple of years I'd been going to a farm not far from home which had animals of every kind, including ponies. I didn't know much about them, but in return for helping out, the farmer would let me have a ride on them now and again. I thought of working in a stables: it was outdoors, I didn't mind ponies and I got on with kids. Looking back now, I think there was also a small fear of working with adults. When I was with kids, I could be a kid, maybe: being small and babyfaced in those days, I thought people wouldn't take me seriously as an adult. I bought *Horse and Hound* magazine, which advertises all types of 'horsey' jobs.

However, I needed money to buy new clothes, not having anything suitable for working outdoors. Much as I disliked office jobs, I took a temporary job as a credit clerk with a catalogue firm which had its offices not far from our house. I hated it, but the money was good. I also worked overtime at nights packing the Christmas orders and within six months I had saved enough to buy the clothes I needed: anorak, jeans and jumpers.

Whilst reading the magazine I saw an advert for stable girls: no pay, except for a couple of pounds' pocket money, bed and board in exchange for all kinds of work and you would be trained in all aspects of horse management with a view to taking exams at the end of the year. It sounded good, but looking back all I can say is my boss definitely got the better bargain! I wrote and was accepted. I gave in my notice, packed my bag, kissed my mum and was off, looking forward to a new experience.

The train snorted and hissed along the tracks, singing a little song: 'This is it, this is it'. The countryside galloped past the windows and the trees waved hello and goodbye in the space of a few seconds. I was leaving home, away to look for adventure and gold-paved streets, not in London, but Wiltshire. Unfortunately all I found was manure-strewn paths. Nevertheless, this was my big day, the day I'd waited for for a long time, impatient and hungry to escape a grim industrial town and find beautiful places. The train eventually arrived, at Shaftesbury station in Dorset, the nearest station to the small village of Semley in Wiltshire. A hulking great, healthy-looking girl approached me. Immediately I felt like a pale-faced townie, which is exactly what I was. She threw me into a Land Rover and drove off into the darkening night. About an hour later we arrived at a small four-roomed cottage, sitting on the brow of the hill, surrounded by sheds, stables and barns. The boss was a stout woman of some seventy years, a Mrs Germaine; the farm girl, her daughter, Lisa, who ran her own farm some miles away. Another healthy-looking girl, my workmate, Carol, sat in the corner of the hearth before a roaring fire. I was given hot, sweet tea and dispatched to bed in a small room behind the kitchen.

I was woken by a shake and a voice calling, 'Six o'clock, time to get up'. I stumbled to the bathroom then fell into my clothes. Breakfast was bigger than any main meal I'd ever seen. I managed to get some down but most of it was beyond me. Later on I learnt to eat more, and even put on a little weight, which cheered Mrs Germaine no end. I was given wellies and dungarees to wear: far too big, not surprising really as most of my clothes came from a shop akin to Mothercare! The first job was to milk the cows. Can you imagine a real townie trying to milk a cow? What a job that was – the cow knows you can't do it and actually holds its milk from you, so you end up on the floor gasping and cursing, whilst the cow licks her lips and flings a crappy tail in your face. Carol gave me a hand as she had already done her two and I was still on half a bucket, if that. My joke about thinking milk only came from bottles was met with such withering scorn that my wellies turned up at the toes. We mucked out the cows and the two horses which were stabled, the rest of the horses being out in the fields. Later on we took hay down to them; there were around twenty-five horses in separate fields around the stables.

There were also goats, sheep, hens, ducks, donkeys, cats and dogs. All of them had to be fed and watered and cleaned up before it was time for the kids to arrive for their lessons. These were boys from a nearby boarding-school who came twice a week, and local kids came out at weekends. During summer five or six caravans were set outside the cottage. Kids from all over the country would stay for a couple of weeks or longer to be trained in how to look after ponies; they would attend gymkhanas and go show-jumping. It was hard and exhausting work, especially in the winter when there was inevitably deep snow, but for all that we had great fun and I was very happy. It was a healthy life: you were up at 6 a.m., worked until 9 p.m. – later sometimes in the summer months – seven days a week. I got on well with Carol and we even managed to chat up two of the local boys who owned motorbikes into taking us for a spin on Sundays when we weren't quite so busy. But social life was really non-existent, the hours were long and all I wanted was a bath at the end of the day and to sleep. At the end of the year we travelled up to London to a posh riding school near Hyde Park to take our horse management exams, the basic-level exams needed to qualify as a riding instructress. We heard a few weeks later that we had passed: it was the first exam I'd taken with much meaning and I was very proud to have survived the year. We could have done more exams, but Mrs Germaine was thinking of selling up, as her daughter wanted her to move into the farm. so we parted. I returned home, healthy and happy, hoping to find a similar job – but one without quite so much hard work.

3

Ireland 1966–70

Today my greatest sense of freedom comes from the knowledge that I can walk where I want, eat what and when I please, sleep as long as I like, bath when I feel like it and light a cigarette that I bought from a shop round the corner. Whenever there are bomb scares in London I become frightened. Not because I have a greater fear of harm than the average individual, but if a department store, station or commercial district is cordoned off and swarming with police officers I fear that I will be associated with the panic. Camden Town, close to where I live and where I shop at Sainsbury's regularly, was the target of a recent bomb attack. Marks & Spencer in Oxford Street was put on alert whilst I was buying some clothes. The sight of the police coming in, rightly protecting the shoppers, terrified me. If I were to be questioned, even now, even after being totally vindicated at the appeal and released, I fear that they would find it – at the very least – an interesting coincidence that I was there.

Some days though, I feel totally armour-plated. I recently heard a story about two members of the Guildford four who were innocently driving along some time after their acquittal and were stopped by police who were doing routine car-checks. As soon as the police realised who they were they were cheerily waved away: the last thing the police want is the adverse publicity of another wrongful arrest or a suggestion of vindictiveness. But I still worry that if I happen to be near the scene of any IRA bombing or scare, my past may make things difficult for me. For every policeman and member of the public who rejoices in my absolution and freedom, there is another who mutters, 'No smoke without fire'.

During these times I think about leaving London. Maybe I should live somewhere more peaceful, somewhere less risky.

Cornwall, perhaps, or Ireland. Some people wonder why I am drawn to Ireland. The main thing is to explain why I like it so much in the first place. After leaving Wiltshire and returning home, I found a job in a private house in the Isle of Man. The work was easy, looking after two hunters and a pony, a temporary job for three months while the regular girl was on holiday. As the months drew to a close I had to think of finding work again. The people who owned the house had recently been on holiday to Ireland. They gave me the brochure of a trekking centre, explaining that the owner had been searching for someone to run the horsey side of the business. I wrote to the owner, Miss Anne O'Conlon, and was invited to take on the job.

When I think back I'm quite astonished at myself. Seventeen years old, quite immature, shy and totally naive, I boarded a boat, with my one suitcase, from Liverpool to Dublin to live with strange people in a strange land. It was quite a shock to me culturally and socially. The accents were different, the language was different, there were signs in Irish everywhere and the people were far friendlier than any I'd met in England. I took a train to Dundalk, a town some fifty miles from Dublin and about eight miles from the border with Northern Ireland. Anne's brother Bill O'Conlon, a handsome man, met me at the station and drove me to Ravensdale, a village about four miles from Dundalk. I was silenced by shyness and the absolute beauty of the surrounding landscape. The village was set at the foot of fat, rolling mountains, with the sea on our left, a rambling forest on the right. Although Ireland is a small island, to me it seemed endless after the narrow streets of Stockport.

Anne's house was large, rambling and Georgian, two storeys high, with a driveway leading through beautiful gardens, complete with stream and pond. The walls were stippled with cream emulsion, there were blue shutters on the windows and pink wisteria climbed to the gables. At the back was a large courtyard with stables and a coach-house adjoining four or five fields that stretched up to the foot of the mountains. It was a place that any tourist would have been delighted to stay in and enjoy.

The first room I entered was the kitchen, large, bright and

airy and filled with people. They were relations of Anne's gathered together for something to eat and drink after returning from Mass, a ritual I soon got used to. At that moment I was totally gobsmacked with a desperate shyness and feeling of alienation, which greatly increased when I was asked if I wanted something to eat. 'A jam buttie will do, thanks.' A moment's silence and then a polite enquiry as to what a 'jam buttie' was. Have you ever wished the floor would swallow you up?! I certainly did. However, it wasn't long before we all started to get used to each other. I was given a room on the second floor and left to unpack.

The next morning after breakfast I started work. My job was to look after the horses; being out in the fields all year round, they mainly looked after themselves. I had to teach children to ride and take guests and visitors on treks in the mountains and forests and down to the beach. It was interesting and varied, I met lots of different French, German, English, American and Irish people, many of whom I'm still in touch with today. It was quite hard work but for the next few years I enjoyed myself there.

Anne, a single woman in her thirties, had inherited the house from her parents. Two old ladies, Bridget and Kitty, also lived there. Bridget was in her seventies. A fat, red-faced lady, she couldn't read or write and had worked for Anne's mother when Anne was a child. Anne had taken her from the county home more as a companion than anything else. Bridget sometimes helped prepare the meals, but mainly she sat in the large kitchen and pottered about. She had a fund of interesting and amusing stories about when she was small, she was deeply religious and lived for the weekends when Anne's brother, Kenneth the priest, came to visit. Kitty, also in her seventies, was more of a mystery. She could read and write beautifully, and had been taught to make the most delicate crochet work, apparently by French nuns, and that was about as much as I knew of her background. She was small and skinny and loved taking a walk down to the corner shop. Kitty had been Bridget's friend in the home, Bridget had missed her company when she same to Ravensdale so Anne had brought Kitty there, too. Anne had two brothers, Bill, who owned a large farm and lived with his family just down the road, and Kenneth the priest, who lived in a parish in Keady, a small town in County Armagh in Northern Ireland. They visited regularly and quite obviously all loved each other very much. This was the first time I'd seen what the term 'family' could really mean, and I was slightly envious. Not that I was an outsider, by any means. I was treated with respect and, I would like to think, eventually, affection.

In that first year I certainly did feel like an outsider. It took me a while to understand the terminology: the 'press' was any cupboard or locker, a 'grape' was a garden fork (a term derived from the word 'grip'). These words and many others came from a curious mixture of dialects and cultures. As Dundalk is only a few miles from the border, dialects from North and South fused into one related to the border areas. It was a time of learning. Most surprising to me was to learn that I was regarded as 'the wee English girl'. It had never crossed my mind to question my identity, but the stress placed on the 'English' certainly got me thinking. I read as much about Ireland and her history as I could, and listened to conversations of old men and women who had suffered at the hands of the dreaded English 'Black and Tans' in the 1920s. Even the children were aware of their history, much more so than a typical English child would be. I had learnt and liked history classes at school, but they were mostly confined to dates and famous people. In Ireland I became aware of a history that was not a dead thing, taught but essentially forgotten, but a force in the present. I formed a sympathy with the Catholics, especially in the North, but this didn't lead towards any burning political commitment. An interest in politics and/or religion was as natural as discussing the weather is in England. It doesn't indicate obsession.

I used to go with Anne into the North on shopping trips. Many items of clothing and foodstuffs were cheaper in the British-subsidised North and lots of people crossed the border to shop. Meat was cheaper, but you weren't allowed to bring it across the border unless certain conditions were met. But so many small roads crisscross the border that the Royal Ulster Constabulary (RUC) and the customs officers found it hard to man, which was good news for those involved in 'smuggling' meat products and other items. Many people's houses were actually sitting on the border, with the front garden in the North and the back in the South. Talk abounded about customs men chasing would-be smugglers through dark and leafy lanes. I met many people from the North, young people of my own age, who told me about aspects of their lives. There was job discrimination if you were a Catholic and great effort was put into changing the voting rules: they wanted 'one man, one vote'. The situation then was that only ratepayers could vote. As there were more Protestant than Catholic ratepayers this meant that very few Catholics were elected to the Northern Irish Parliament, so the Catholics felt they were under-represented. I was slightly bemused and outraged by all this information; the fact that your religious faith could hinder you getting work was a notion I'd never encountered before. My journeys to the North, which is beautiful in parts, were always slightly tinged with unease, the idea that something was not quite right. There was an air of ever-increasing tension in the months leading up to 1969 and the civil rights marches.

When I'd been in Ireland for about two years, I returned home for a visit. My mother had remarried shortly after I went to Ireland. My stepfather, Sam, is some years younger than my mother. He appeared to be a good man and I was glad for my mother's sake. It couldn't have been easy for him taking on a ready-made family, but he did a great job and I'm grateful to him for all the support he has given my mother over the years and the way he has supported me too. After they married, they moved house. It was strange to be in a new home with a new dad. I knew no one in the area and didn't feel at all settled. To be truthful, I was glad to get back to Ireland. I began to feel restless and unsure about where I was going in life. I had learnt something about Ireland and I began to realise that there were hundreds more countries and cultures I'd never experienced. I loved Ravensdale, but there was something in me that felt I was missing out. On what, I had no idea.

During the years 1967 to 1969 events in Northern Ireland and abroad reflected a distinct air of change, restlessness and unease, a questioning of values. America became involved in

Vietnam, there were civil rights marches in Alabama. Che Guevara was killed in Bolivia. Martin Luther King was assassinated. Students marched and fought police in France and Italy. Millions in the US had demonstrated against the Vietnam War. In Northern Ireland, a civil rights association was set up; Republican clubs were banned; thousands of students took to the streets in protest. Civil rights marchers were attacked and beaten by Loyalists and even members of the RUC on their way from Belfast to Derry. In April 1969, the twenty-one-year old Bernadette Devlin had been elected MP. The Battle of Bogside, in which hundreds of loyalists attacked Catholic homes in Derry, had been fought; the Catholic ghettos in Belfast had also been attacked, the British Army moved in and the Provisional IRA was formed.

I was going through my own crisis at the time. A few years earlier, Anne had decided it was time for me to learn how to drive. I was all for the idea and she set about teaching me, but she was such a back-seat driver the two of us were nervous wrecks after the first hour. We decided someone else should do the teaching, and Anne suggested John, the foreman on her brother's farm. I knew him well enough to chat to, he was single, about twelve years older than me and a very likeable man. In the evenings we would drive off around the country lanes in his car; he was a very good teacher. The driving lessons developed into going into town to the pictures, or driving somewhere for a meal. One night as we returned from our usual evening out, he proposed marriage. I was totally amazed. I liked him immensely, and now suppose I loved him too, but I was immature sexually, I'd never 'dated', never been kissed in any way except with non-erotic affection. I said I would think about it, pleased that someone loved me as much as that. I told Anne, who being the matchmaker she was, thought it was great and immediately started talking arrangements. For the next few weeks, events and people took over my life. It seemed like the whole village had known this would happen, except me, and I felt as if I had been manoeuvred into a position I wasn't quite sure I wanted. I needed time to think about it, to talk to someone, but I was too immature and insecure to really know what I wanted and far too shy to stand there and say,

'Hold on a minute, let's talk about this.' The thought of asserting myself and perhaps arguing didn't come into it: I couldn't bear arguing and would do anything rather than get involved in any dispute. I think I was also slightly afraid of the thought of sex. As talk turned into engagement rings and house-hunting, I realised I wasn't ready for this kind of commitment, so, bewildered, panic-stricken and with an ignorance that must have seemed totally ungrateful, I bolted, legged it, and left John sitting over a cup of coffee.

Much as I enjoyed my work, particularly with the children whom I'd taught to ride and the treks through the gorgeous countryside; much as I thought I valued the friendships I'd made – with a French girl, Anne Yvonne, from Brittany, who was teaching in a small school across the border and who has supported me through all the long years in prison, with Polly from Dublin, with all the people I knew in the village – I couldn't handle the idea of settling down. I've never regretted not getting married, but I am sorry that I didn't have the maturity to handle the situation and deeply regret the effect it must have had on John, more so than anyone. In retrospect, I think that the events which were then happening, the changes, the restlessness, also affected me. I was beginning to feel that I wanted something else and had fallen into a depression of mind, which resulted in confusion. My actions were totally illogical, but feeling the way I did, logic didn't come into it.

I went back to Stockport. It was awful, I felt depressed and guilty and my self-esteem was pretty low. I got a job in Woolworth's: it was boring and dull, as was my social life. It was a stressful period and there were times when I thought I was going to crack up. I suppose it was difficult for my parents, having me hanging around. It was certainly hard for me to try and adjust to their lifestyle. I decided to run again, only this time it was into the army.

4

Army, Ireland, Arrest 1970–74

Some people have thought it strange that I joined the army in the context of the situation in Northern Ireland. However, in 1970–71 the army was not really viewed as an 'enemy': the majority of people were glad it had moved in and stopped the attacks by Loyalist gangs on Catholic ghettos. My brother had been in the army and my mother had served in the ATS during the war, so the idea of joining up wasn't really an alien thought. It was also a different enough lifestyle to attract me.

I was sent first to Guildford for nine weeks' basic training. It was the type of marching, fold your blankets, stand by your beds routines that most civilians view as typical of army life. During this period, I was assessed and tested for signals training. I was then sent to Catterick, a garrison town in Yorkshire, for the next four months, learning how to become a 'communications centre operator'. Sounds very grand, doesn't it? We attended classes during weekdays and spent weekends walking on the moors, or exploring the nearby town of Richmond, a beautiful place. It was like being in a college and much of the routine was passed over in favour of teaching. I learnt how to send and receive messages via phone and telex, where the messages were sent, and other things, such as how to recognise a 'staff car', which might contain some important personage, and of course how to salute him or her as they passed. At the end of four months we sat examinations and a couple of weeks later I found that I had passed. Amidst general celebration we received our signals badge, nicknamed 'jimmies'; it was a silver soldier holding up a globe. I had enjoyed the training: it was interesting and good fun at times. Being viewed as 'students' allowed us to be totally foolish and silly and to behave somewhat immaturely at times, sometimes a novelty for me.

Getting drunk, even stealing and driving off one or two of the tanks across the moors, although frowned on, was seen as a natural outburst.

Training over, we waited for our posting to begin work. The posting could be to anywhere in the world where the army is stationed and we were encouraged to apply to stations we fancied, but the truth is you rarely get it. I applied for Cyprus and Germany, I got Aldershot. If you've ever been to Aldershot, you'll probably understand why I wasn't at all happy. It was horrible. Aldershot must rate as one of the most boring towns in England. The main Parachute Regiment is stationed there, with hundreds of fellas who just love telling you how brave they were. The female quarters were at the centre of the station and we were heavily outnumbered by the men, many of whom made it plain that we were there only to satisfy their sexual appetites and that the sight of that coveted red beret was supposed to make us swoon at their feet, or on their beds, whichever was more convenient! The female barracks were quite comfortable and clean. Four of us shared a large room. As we were all Signal personnel on shift work it was rare for us all to be in the room together for any length of time, so we didn't live on top of each other, which was quite pleasant. The regimentation and drilling which had dominated life in Guildford, and to some extent Catterick, was bypassed here.

Working hours were varied, 8 a.m. to 6 p.m. some days, then 2 p.m. to 10 p.m. or 8 p.m. to 8 a.m. Social life had to be fitted in: usually we spent off-duty hours in the mess or watching TV. Days off and weekends free were spent travelling to London: Aldershot was not the place for off-duty hours. Although the work was interesting, the environment and atmosphere began to wear me down: some of the officers thought that if your hair touched your collar the might of the British Empire would collapse. So, after a few months I requested a posting elsewhere. I was given the excruciating choice of Hounslow or Salisbury, both places I'd heard were the same, if not worse, than Aldershot. So much for thoughts of wicked Berlin or steaming Limassol.

So, one weekend, having received a pass, I did a runner and went AWOL. I went home to my parents, but not for long. I knew the police would be sent there to look for me, so I jumped on the first boat to Dublin, out of their reach. For a while I returned to Anne and Ravensdale, but still I felt unsettled and that I wasn't totally forgiven; I was still a little ashamed about running off and leaving John and upsetting everyone. I left Ravensdale and went to Dublin.

From this period on I began to drift. With no real money and no aim or goal to work towards, I entered a period of uncertainty and doubt. I met two young people of my own age, Dan and Mary, who were selling the republican newspaper, *An Phoblacht*. After chatting for a while, they suggested I should sell some too, to earn some money, which I agreed might be handy. I spent a day or two a week on this. I moved into a house, sectioned off into flats, in the Sandymount area of Dublin. It was full of young people who spent their days consuming vast amounts of coffee and discussing the wrongs of the world. Some of them were students; some, like me, had drifted in; some were vociferously political, an amalgamation of anarchists, socialists and communists. We swapped ideas, attended public meetings and demonstrations and probably thought we were the voice of discontent and righteousness. Many drifted off and back again as I did myself. I travelled the north and south of Ireland, sometimes with people, sometimes not, drifting around, sleeping rough, probably unwashed, thumbing lifts, always hungry.

It was probably during this period that I began to sink into a severe depression. It's hard for me now to assess the state I was in – memories of so long ago are vague, unpleasant feelings and emotions abound. It was not a happy time, of that I'm sure. I was questioned by the RUC during this period and it has been said that I made some pretty weird statements. I can believe it. To begin with I was AWOL and so I didn't use my real name for fear of arrest, often I fabricated a lifestyle in an attempt to dissuade them from enquiring into my real background. I should have told them who I was, but the fear of prison then was much greater than it is now. I was viewed as 'undesirable', and put back on a boat to England. I thought I might as well go and give myself up to the army. I didn't know what would happen, but I had no other choice.

I went to the police station in Stockport and said I'd come

to give myself up. The desk sergeant thought I'd run away from home. Although I was twenty-two, being small and looking young, I wasn't really surprised. After some explanation I was given a travel warrant and the following day took the train to Aldershot. On arrival I was confined to barracks for a week, then two policemen in civilian clothes (who could have been Army Intelligence, I'm not sure) interviewed me about my movements in Northern Ireland. I gave them as much information as I could. It wasn't much, I don't know if what I said made sense or not, but anyway they seemed indifferent and I was then discharged from the army. They told me I was due some back pay: if you went AWOL a percentage of your pay was kept for you. If I'd known, I would have stayed away longer. I travelled to my parents' house and a few days later received £250, a hundred of which I gave to my mother.

It was now late in 1972. I spent the next few months or so working at odd jobs in places like Woolworth's again. I still felt unsettled and slightly unhappy, had made few friends and had little or no social life. I returned to Dublin a couple of times and visited people I knew in the North.

In August 1973 I went to London and got a live-in job as chambermaid in a hotel in the Elephant and Castle district. I shared a room with another girl, Elaine. We became friendly and usually spent our free time together. The work wasn't hard by any means. From 9 a.m. to 3 p.m. six days a week our job was to make sure the rooms were clean and tidy. It was interesting in that we met people from all over the world, and was quite lucrative with the tips we received. On one of my days off I went to Kilburn to meet a friend, Jack, who had recently moved there from Dublin. Over drinks at the pub, he told me he had joined Sinn Fein, an Irish political party, which was not at that time a well-known organisation and not banned from broadcasting, as it is now. I said I'd come and see what the crack was. A few nights later I went along to a meeting held in a second-floor room above a pub. The main topic of discussion was the situation in Northern Ireland, and there were leaflets and books for sale. At that time, there was a bombing campaign going on in England and of course this was also discussed. I would like to say here that many Sinn Fein members do not approve of bombing campaigns; they believe, as I do, that it is only politically, by discussion involving all parties in Northern Ireland, that a resolution of the problem will come about. We attended public meetings and demonstrations and held vigils, one in particular outside Brixton prison where the Price sisters were being held. They were on hunger strike in protest against not being allowed to serve their sentence in a prison in Northern Ireland, a protest every prisoner serving time far from home would agree with, I'm sure.

On 10 September a bomb exploded in the railway bar at Euston station. It was a Monday. Elaine and I had the day off work. We'd decided to go to the pictures to see *High Plains Drifter* starring Clint Eastwood, a violent and moody western. On leaving the cinema, we heard about the Euston bomb. Probably urged by the curiosity that makes many people appear at such scenes, Elaine and I decided to go and see what had happened, so we got on the tube. Surprisingly, the station was not cordoned off; many people were in the bar and restaurant, drinking and talking. Apparently the bomb had been small, containing 2lb. and 5lb. of nitroglycerine-based explosive and about a dozen people had been injured. We bought a drink and sat down between two or three lads. Elaine chatted to the ones on her right and I talked to the guy next to me. He was from Belfast, he told me, and was waiting to catch the train to Heysham. He offered to buy me a drink and I agreed; after a while he went to buy us another drink. While he was at the bar I played a quick game on the fruit machine in the corner. Turning round, I saw the man surrounded by another three men, obviously in some sort of trouble. Not wanting to get involved, Elaine and I decided to leave. At the door, we were stopped by a fourth man, who identified himself as a policeman and asked us to go with him. For the record I would like to say I was not drunk and shouting, as stated by some policeman. The only reason Elaine and I were stopped that day was because we were in the company of this guy from Belfast, who had been under observation for some time.

We were taken into the police office on the station and placed in separate rooms, then questioned about our movements. I told them I had been to the cinema and listed the day's activities; they checked with Elaine and seemed quite satisfied. I was asked about the man I was talking to, but could only tell them that he said he was from Belfast and was waiting for a train. We were held for about two or three hours while the police checked and compared our stories. We heard from the housekeeper the next day that they had questioned her and she had told them she had met us leaving the hotel and what time, which was of crucial importance, as the time we left the hotel was the same time as the bomb exploded. Later that evening the police asked if they could 'swab' our hands, that is, wipe our hands with dry cotton wool, then wet them with a solution and wipe them again. They were testing to see if we had been in contact with any explosive substance. Throughout the evening they were very calm and courteous, not at all like the police I encountered after that. Half an hour later they said we could go. Elaine and I left together; I didn't see the man from Belfast leave, but heard later that he was also released that evening.

We never found out the results of that testing for explosives. Knowing that we hadn't been in contact with any we didn't worry about it. It is important to explain here the results of the tests in light of forthcoming events. Each of us were swabbed six times, with the following results:

Belfast man: 4 positive results and two trace results
Elaine: 5 trace results and one negative result
Myself: 4 negative results and two faint trace results

This meant that the man from Belfast could have been handling explosives, Elaine might have, but it was unlikely, and I probably had not. The two faint trace results, according to forensic experts, were not an indication of handling explosives and could not be determined as a positive result. They were likely to be either contamination as a result of handling debris or more realistically, the result of contact between myself and the Belfast man – we had shaken hands and I had then handled a glass which he had first touched. At trial, these results were never revealed in their entirety and all were described as 'positive', a move which the Appeal Court judges described as, 'lamentable omissions'. The forensic experts, had, in the court's view, 'taken the law into their own hands, and concealed from the prosecution, the defence and the court, matters which might have changed the course of the trial' and they had 'placed a false and distorted scientific picture before the jury'.

Although these results were later described as 'positive' at the 1974 trial, the events immediately after the 1973 Euston bombing negate this description. The results were known to the police the day after Euston. If they were satisfied these results were positive and that I had handled explosives, why then was I not arrested and questioned? I stayed in London for a few more months, at the same hotel, but was never questioned again. Furthermore, if my results were positive, and Elaine's and the Belfast man's even more so, why were they not arrested in either 1973 or 1974?

I remained in London until around November 1973, working at the hotel. I didn't want to spend the rest of my days as a chambermaid: I felt there was something lacking in life. I was finally given the boot by the housekeeper after playing a practical joke on her. It was time to move on.

Back in Stockport I found a job in a local café – not very exciting, but it was work. Just before Christmas 1973 I was reading the newspaper and saw an advertisement for work which seemed to offer a glimmer of excitement to brighten my dull existence. Chipperfield's circus had arrived at a place called BelleVue in Manchester and were looking for a girl to help with the horses. Here was something different. I applied and was accepted. I lived in a caravan with Julie, who also worked with the horses. Our job was to look after about twelve horses and prepare them for the show each day. We also sold programmes and did other odd jobs when the show was on. The horses were large rosin-backs, which means they have a very wide back suitable for performers doing stunts. They were grey, with large black spots, quite attractive. There has been a lot of disquiet regarding the treatment of circus animals, but all I can say is that they appeared to be well treated and well looked after. Unfortunately animals such as the big cats were confined to cages, and the elephants were tethered all the time, but all of them were well fed.

The circus is a very transitory life. Workers come and go

with each town and the constant travelling for most of the year makes it something to be avoided for those seeking a stable life. It is, though, very lively. The only thing that matters is the show, and everyone is put to work to ensure that all goes well. It wasn't hard work by any means, it was fun and different and I enjoyed working with such personalities. I also enjoyed the shows: it was good to see all the kids getting a real buzz out of it. Many came round to see the horses and inevitably asked how we got the spots on them! We always said it was a hell of a job painting them on every night. Life with the circus was rough at times – living in a caravan, nowhere to bathe properly, going to the launderette with your clothes. I sometimes think all circus people are caught up in an illusion, sometimes shattered by the tawdry glamour, unfunny clowns, backstage arguments and basic living conditions. In January the circus packed up, a lengthy, arduous task, and moved on to Chipping Norton in Oxfordshire, where the winter quarters were, to rest up and repair ready for the summer season starting in April or May. I didn't see the point in staying till then; I wasn't about to make a lifelong commitment so, along with many others, I left.

I travelled to London and met another girl and two fellas who were wandering too. We hung around together for a while. Today, we would be called 'homeless', then I think we were just dossers: no money, no shelter, no idea what we were going to do and not really bothered, living in apathy. We climbed over walls and sneaked past railway guards to sleep on goods trains at night, most of them unlocked. For all I know homeless people still do this, it's a lot more comfortable than a cardboard box in a doorway on the Strand, that's for sure. By day, the fellas would go off and nick food or try and make some money, by what means, I never knew. One night we slept on a goods train and the following day left the baggage there whilst we wandered off. On returning that night, we discovered the goods train had left for points north, along with our stuff. It says much about our attitudes that we weren't really bothered; in fact, if the train had left with us sleeping on it, I don't think we would have minded too much. If possessions were unimportant, money wasn't.

If we had money, we used the station loo to clean up in; if we didn't, we stayed unwashed. Some days we ate, some days we didn't. We must have been a motley lot to look at. Living like that is a vicious circle, no one will give you a job, and you can't claim social security as you need an address. The longer you live it, the more you sink into abject apathy, your self-esteem and pride decrease until you get to the point of indifference. Who cares anyway?

One of the guys Eddie, decided he was going to hitch up to Cardiff, where he had friends. I decided to go with him. Why not? I wasn't doing anything important. We got lifts along the way, mainly from lorry-drivers, and arrived in Cardiff at around 8 p.m. Eddie, having a bit of money, got us a room in a bed and breakfast place. We shared the bed, which was glorious after all those nights of sleeping rough. The next day, Eddie said he was going off to see his mates and would meet me later. I wandered round, unimpressed. Cardiff appeared bleak and the weather was wet and grey. Eddie never turned up. I waited and waited. Finally I found out, some months later, that he had been arrested for shoplifting or some such. Eventually I left the town and started to hitch. I had a vague idea that I would go to Liverpool, I knew a friend of a friend there. I got a lift from a young guy in a sports car, who offered me a joint. I took it and escaped for a while into a rosy glow. It was 14 February 1974 and, although I didn't know it, the start of the real nightmare was only a few hours away. A large, dark blue van appeared round the corner . . .

5

Remand and Trial, 1974

On the evening of Monday, 18 February 1974 I was charged with conspiracy to cause an explosion on the M62 motorway in Yorkshire. On 4 February a bomb in an army coach had killed twelve people. I was also charged with the murder of one of the twelve people who had died in that explosion. In the following weeks I would be charged with conspiracy to cause an explosion at Euston station in September 1973 and another at Latimer College in Buckinghamshire, also with another eleven murders from the M62 coach.

I was taken from Wakefield to Dewsbury Magistrate's Court for remand that night. It was an old courthouse, due to be demolished, bleak and grey. There I was placed in a cell, supposedly to sleep, but I was not to that night. The door was left open, on the orders of a senior policeman. The cell looked out on to a grey soulless corridor, where four or five policemen and women sat chatting, wondering who was this strange person they had to keep company during the black hours. They brought me sandwiches and mugs of hot, sweet tea and we spent the night sitting around a table, playing cards.

Does this convey to you the idea of how a supposed IRA bomber should be treated? Probably not, and the reason was that these men, certainly those in charge, knew that I wasn't the one – but I was available, stupid enough to go along with them, past caring what happened to me. They also had the forensic 'evidence' which proved I had been in contact with explosive substances: the tests for the presence of nitroglycerine, from the swabs taken from my hands earlier. This evidence had been offered by a forensic scientist. It was later stated by the Appeal Court that these tests were, 'of no value in establishing contact between the appellant and explosives in 1974'. And that, if the trial judge had known . . . he would have excluded the evidence as valueless.

Other forensic evidence offered by the Prosecution scientists were claims of positive traces of nitroglycerine found on swabs taken from the floor of the caravan I had been living in whilst working with the circus. They also stated that positive traces had been taken from my hands after the incident at Euston station and, of course, there was Dr Skuse's evidence that positive traces had been taken from my hands. It emerged eighteen years later that these scientists had failed to produce vital evidence relating to these tests which showed that the most likely origin had been floor polish on the floor of the caravan and soap traces on my hands. They also concealed evidence of tests done the day before the trial started which showed that innocent contamination could have come from touching debris at Euston station or from contact with others who may themselves have been contaminated.

The next morning I appeared in Dewsbury Magistrate's Court. A court session is supposed to be a place where you seek justice and can ask for whatever help you need. In fact, all you are allowed to do is to answer yes or no to the few questions they put to you, such as 'You are Judith Ward?' The only time you get to say anything other than yea or nay is when they ask whether you plead 'Guilty' or 'Not guilty'. The answer to that is 'Not guilty'. I didn't have a solicitor and hadn't a clue what was going on; I was tired and weary of questions anyway. I was then remanded to Risley Remand Centre.

Risley – 'Grisly Risley' was its nickname, I later found – is a low, sprawling building, divided into two sections, one for males and one for females, each with its own perimeter fence and surrounded by a high, redbrick wall. The inside is dreary and cold, the walls painted an institutional dirty yellow or green. I was taken into the reception area, strip-searched, washed (to my great relief) and then 'did my property'. This is where you sit in an office and a prison officer writes on a card a list of all your belongings, anything and everything you have on you or with you. The officer then takes away certain articles which are not allowed. As I only had the clothes I stood up in, which weren't mine anyway, my 'property check' was done quickly. I was then taken to a cell on the hospital wing. The cell was about 9 feet by 6 feet with a bed, a table and a chair. The ubiquitous potty was under the bed, there was no integral sanitation: Britain's prisons are not noted for being part of the twentieth century. The view from the barred window was of a large area, which turned out to be the exercise yard, to my left and opposite were more cells, and to the right was the fence and the wall, over the top of which a few trees waved. I was left alone here for the rest of the day and evening, with occasionally a face peering in at me through the small window in the centre of the door. I slept most of that day, glad to be away from the world, not realising that this isolation was to wreak havoc on my already chaotic mind and send me into another time and space, from which it would take years to return.

The following day, after a really revolting meal called 'breakfast', I was moved from this cell to another. To gain entry you had to walk along the main corridor, enter a locked door into an annexe of the main prison in which was situated a small corridor leading to two cells. These were the punishment cells, usually inhabited by inmates considered recalcitrant, who had broken the prison rules in some way. I was on the second floor. Below me were more punishment cells and strip cells. My cell was brick-faced, dirty yellow, with a high window at the top of the outside wall and adjoining the ceiling. I had to climb up on the bed to look out. The window was barred in such a way that in summer it wouldn't open more than a few inches. The only furniture was a table and a bed, a strange-looking effort reaching only six inches from the floor. A bed for those who suffered from epileptic fits, I found out, so they wouldn't harm themselves if they fell out. Of course the potty was there too, a companion to accompany my loss of pride and self-esteem and a constant reminder of degradation and humiliation. I existed in this cell for nearly eleven months.

I say existed, as I certainly wasn't living in any real sense. I was on 'Rule 43', a prison rule under which prisoners are placed for reasons of 'good order and discipline' or as a 'protection from other prisoners'. I was never quite sure under

which definition I came. Not that it mattered to me, I didn't
even know I was under this rule until I was transferred to
Durham. My mind was blank, I was emotionless, uncaring.
If they said 'Do it' I did it. Although I didn't realise it, my
family were aware by now of my plight and they appointed a
solicitor to represent me. He was a good, caring man and
tried his best to undertake what must have seemed a gargan-
tuan task, with little to go on because of evidence
undisclosed. He asked questions and more questions, I
answered or didn't as the case might be, as I sank into my
apathy, my grave new world. It was safe in there, no one
could touch me. I would stay locked in my indifference.

I had few visits. My mother came once. It was dreadful: I
didn't know what to say and neither did she. The visit lasted
just fifteen minutes – what can you say when you only have
fifteen minutes? I was allowed to write letters, but wrote few;
it was as if the outside world now had no meaning. I was not
permitted to associate with any other prisoners, although I
could sometimes hear shouted conversations echoing
through the bars at night. The isolation and lack of com-
munication pushed me further into retreat. I had got to the
stage where if an officer entered my cell with a meal I
wouldn't even notice she had been until I found a cold, con-
gealed mess on a plate some hours later. My moods swayed
between high hysteria, when I found I would sing for hours
and laugh at nothing, and times when I wouldn't utter a
word all day as I read book after book, retaining nothing.
Then there were depressions, black, foul, soul-destroying. I
wanted to lie down and die, never wake up. I cried at
nothing and everything: prisoners talking to each other
through the bars at night, a bird singing in the early dawn,
disturbed prisoners crying in the cells below.

During this time, I had been experiencing severe abdomi-
nal pain and, shortly after the doctor examined me, it was
decided that I needed an appendectomy. I was taken out of
Risley around 8 a.m. one morning, amidst great secrecy and
security, to Warrington General Hospital to have the operation. There was a slight argument in the pre-op. room
between the surgeon and the plain-clothes police, who
wanted to accompany my drugged and inert body into the

theatre. They obviously thought I was no mere mortal and could 'do a runner' quite easily, completely unhindered by any amount of anaesthetic. The surgeon was not happy about it and refused to continue unless they waited outside. I presume they did, as the operation went ahead. In the 1970s it was considered sound practice to keep a patient in hospital for up to five days after an appendix operation, as the Appeal Court Judge pointed out, quite shocked by the evidence of my 'aftercare' that day. I was shaken vigorously to ascertain that I had recovered slightly from the anaesthetic, carried down to the ambulance and whisked back to Risley. The whole process, including operation, had taken something like fifty minutes. I was then placed in a staff rest-room adjoining the prison hospital for my convalescence.

Although I remember this incident, most of my remand period remains a blur. When I think of it, a great melancholy fills me. I have lost nearly twelve months of my life, all that remains is emotion – heaving, gut-tearing emotion, sadness – a giant tear lies in my soul which can never be shed without feelings of intense loneliness and fear. Yes, I was scared. What was happening to me? Everyone wanted answers and no one wanted to know. I cried for three days one time – I woke and was crying and couldn't stop. I don't know why, couldn't tell anyone why. The doctor came and gave me medicine, clear and innocent looking with a lingering foul taste. I slept, I woke, more medicine, more sleep and so it went on, until one day I woke up and wasn't crying any more. I tried to cut my wrists with a small piece of metal I found in the loo, perhaps left there by some inmate with the thought of doing the same thing. It didn't work, so a few weeks later I tried again with a sharpened needle I found lodged in the table drawer. I understood nobody and nothing and they didn't bother to understand me. I was a confusion of wants: I wanted someone to talk to, but didn't want to talk to those who came to see me; I wanted someone to explain, but didn't want to listen. So it went on. Days dragged by, winter to spring to summer to autumn – to trial.

October 1974. I was bundled into a van at some ungodly hour in the morning, alongside three female prison officers. Escorted by two cars full of gun-toting detectives and two outriders on motorbikes, we made out way to Wakefield Crown Court. Sirens screaming, lights flashing, we roared up the motorway, ignoring the early-morning drivers. Screeching along the outside lane, we arrived quite easily at the courthouse, or rather the police station across the road. This police station was to be 'home' for the next four to five weeks, except for weekends when we returned to Risley. We had an annexe all to ourselves: kitchen, living-room, bathroom and two cells, all mod cons. My guards were perplexed by this, and unsure how to react, they spent the following weeks alternately friendly and distant in approach.

Later that morning we moved to the court, police guarding all the surrounding buildings, marksmen on the roof, the local telephone kiosk padlocked 'temporarily out of use'. Court officials and pressmen produced passes, visitors were submitted to stringent searches before being allowed entry. The cell had cream walls, a tiny, high window, a bench fixed to the wall and a barrel ceiling like a vault, clean, cold and characterless.

Everyone there must have been overwhelmed and fearful as the trial progressed to witness ranks of police marching up the street in a formidable show of strength. Throughout the trial there were numerous hoax bomb alerts and the court had to be cleared many times. How could any one reach a neutral verdict in such an atmosphere, especially when two pubs in Guildford were bombed?

Into the dock, traditional like on TV. Bewigged men, mountains of paper, jury members curious and alert, press with pens poised, me, sitting on a chair placed on a box because I'm too small to see over the dock wall. I didn't want to see anyway, didn't want to be there, I wasn't really, only my physical form, my head gone away, retired, retreated, redundant. They're not talking about me, this is not me, I'm not listening, I'll sit here and draw pictures. Is this really happening, are they stupid, am I stupid, who cares anyway, the book is written, you're only the character. What's that? They want you to go in the witness box and speak? No, I can't do this, what do I say? Say anything, it doesn't matter anyway, and so I did, said anything and nothing, they're not listening anyway, except for the sensational, the claims of bombing, the 'marriage' to a young man who had been killed whilst on active service for the IRA. Why did I say that? I don't know, don't even know where his name came from, it has been said that it was suggested earlier but I have no memory of this. All I can say is that this is a pointer to the mental state I was in; it was just one of the many absurd statements I made at the time. I said I didn't do it, yes, I know I confessed but that was to get them off my back, don't you understand? Maybe you still think they're all Dixons of Dock Green.

Over the next few weeks evidence was heard of my attendance at demonstrations, my selling of 'political' newspapers. Photographs were produced to support the evidence, all viewed as pretty damning. I was political, therefore a revolutionary. All this contributed to the 'guilt by association' alluded to by my barrister. So the evidence seems irrefutable. The undisclosed evidence, consisting of statements and forensic tests, lies hidden from judge, jury and defence. The police and their forensic experts sit silent and condemnatory. Regarded as paragons of virtue, no one knows they have papers hidden away, of the evidence indicating a great deal of doubt, rather than a sure certainty. Of the prison medical reports containing such statements as; '[she] is unfit to plead . . . her life is in some danger . . . we have an acute psychiatric emergency on our hands'. No, they don't want these issues raised: a severely distraught woman in the throes of 'an acute psychotic depression' isn't consistent with their idea of a cold-blooded, murdering terrorist. They don't want the evidence of these reports, the discussions recorded on paper of the 'political implications and dangers of the defendant's illness and possible death, and the need to be prepared for a possible leakage of information'; withholding the evidence seems the thing to do. After all, this information might damage the prosecution case.

I sit there blankly, defeated by the righteousness of these people. How can I fight them – all these strong, powerful people – by myself? Unknowledgeable, ignorant, I have a defence who are totally uninformed about what has been said or done. I sit apart, I am a part, I am parts, little pieces.

Thus, after some three hours of deliberating by the jury, I was found guilty on all counts, judgment was passed on the 'gun-runner, intelligence officer, bomb carrier, bomb-maker'. Thirty years and twelve life sentences seemed a nice round figure, with the eight months spent on remand kindly taken into account. Did I cry, did I scream my innocence, did I curse? No, I did and said nothing. I was nothing, a statue, an unthinking robot dead from the neck up; except in my inner time and space where everyone was good to everyone else and the world was defined in bright primary colours and it was much easier to function in there away from the sharp contrasts of the black and white law courts and prison cells.

I returned to Grisly Risley into the womb of Victorian ethics and ideals, my cosy semi-detached cell for another month, until one morning I was abruptly woken and transferred noisily to H Wing in Her Majesty's Prison, Durham.

It must be remembered that I was tried during a rather odd political climate and that the public, the judge, the newspapers, and most of all the jury, had been reading about this thing called 'terrorism' almost every day for several years. By no means was it all IRA related. The headlines about Entebbe, the Baader-Meinhof group, the PLO, the not-too-distant memory of the Paris Commune of 1968, when Daniel Cohn Bendit and his group threatened the political stability of France, let alone the activities of the Angry Brigade in England during the early seventies had all conspired to make people think that the world was no longer the safe and peaceful planet that it had appeared to be ten years earlier. 'Terrorism' was a word frequently used but seldom understood. Anyone who was up on such a charge (although at the time of my trial 'terrorism' had yet to officially enter the statute books as a crime), was somehow associated with all those other disturbing people, places and events. Britain was beginning to panic about the escalation of IRA activity and the police force was anxious to prove that it was in control. The evil eye was cast upon the Irish and anyone associated with them, and numbers of us became scapegoats.

6

Durham 1974–76

Some time in the early 1970s a middle-aged, bearded folk singer had a hit record which concerned his misery about having to leave Durham. One thing is sure: if I was ever asked to choose my Desert Island Discs, this song would not be one of them. I spent nearly fifteen and a half years of my life in Durham. I'm told it's a beautiful city with a mystical Celtic history, but I was not sorry to leave old Durham town.

The prison is a large, Victorian edifice, built from quarry stone, blacked in colour over the years, soulless in appearance. It houses some 1,000 male inmates in separate wings each containing maybe a hundred men.

E Wing was one of these wings, housing at various times such notorious inmates as the Great Train Robbers, the Krays and Ian Brady. It was closed down in 1972, deemed unfit for its male prisoners following internal protests and riots. It was reopened in 1974 (at the cost of untold thousands of pounds, mainly spent on security), deemed fit for female inmates and became known as H Wing. Victorian in look as well as ideas, it was built in the shape of a narrow 'L', four storeys high. Inside, its brick walls were thickly painted in revolting shades of yellow and green. Suicide nets stretched across each landing to prevent the inmates performing desperate acts of kamikaze.

The cells have high ceilings and measure approximately 9 feet by 5 feet, and even that may be an exaggeration. Each had the usual potty under the bed, bucket and bowl in the corner, all ablutions catered for. There was a wooden wardrobe and a locker which had a drawer and a little cupboard on each side of it and a small, metal-framed wood chair placed alongside it. Small wood-framed mirrors were screwed on to the walls alongside small wood-framed cork boards for photos. The furniture was old, some of it falling to bits. Wardrobes had doors hanging off, locker drawers were missing. The pots had all too obviously been used many times before. Bedcovers were of a rough material, drab green, pillows were in short supply, towels were a greyish-white, thin and worn, ripped in places. The old-fashioned, heavy doors were reinforced with metal sheeting, painted grey and slammed with finality. Their heavy-duty locks needed over-sized keys, and they had small invasive spy-holes. There was very little natural daylight and too much glare from fluorescent strip-lighting. It was clean, compact and claustrophobic. We froze in summer as the thick walls refused to take in the heat of the sun; we boiled in winter with heating that flowed in through wall-ducts and was uncontrollable.

The outside doors were controlled by remote control, and the whole wing was surrounded by a 20-foot-high wire perimeter fence, topped in places by swirls of razor-sharp barbed wire. Cameras were placed strategically round the tarmacked exercise area, which has an uninspiring view of the outside wall, that is even higher than the fence – no Peeping Toms here, except maybe the cameramen. The 'church', which was used by all denominations, was actually two small cells knocked into one on the ground floor, which is termed 'the flat'. The workroom had fluorescent lighting and a few windows with thick bottle glass to 'protect our privacy' and our skins from the harsh glare of daylight. To one side were two rows of old-fashioned sewing machines which Singer probably gave away in the First World War. The room's sharp pointed roof was made up of windows, which were later whitewashed over because of the heat. No air conditioning here. Access to the workroom was through a corridor leading from the wing, with cameras making sure you were in step. An inside area, prettily named 'the blue room', had nothing pretty about it with its concrete floor, four brick walls and two floodlights, one not working. There was barbed wire near the roof, where chinks of daylight fought to glare at us through two dirty, bottle-glass windows. Covering all was a blue plastic corrugated roof, hence the name. When it rained a large pool of water formed in the far corner where the drains overflowed. Rating in the good cowshed guide – nil.

The 'flat', or ground floor, is where all the admin. offices are located, alongside the church, a bathroom, a kitchen (for washing-up only), a 'recess' comprising large sluice, sink and toilet, one on each landing. In all, there were only seven toilets on the wing for thirty-nine women. On the far end of the L shape a door leads into another wing for male inmates (never to be opened when females are lurking about); at the other end a barred, remote-control gate leads into a small corridor. On the left of this is the visiting room comprising two tables and suitable amount of chairs and one large desk for the staff to oversee the visits. Two large, bright windows look out on to a wall. On the right another door leads into a small corridor, on the left of which is another room where suspect visitors are searched, and the 'property room' where all belongings not considered necessary to prison life are stored. Here too the outer door of the wing leads to a small fenced area, which in turns leads to the main prison. Access to this is through a small gate in the fence overlooked by cameras. Back in the wing opposite the gate is the 'security room', which can be viewed through a small shaded window. This is where the TVs, which capture our every movement outside the confines of the wing, are stored. Several male staff and a few females work in here.

The second and third landings are mainly cell accommodation (room for thirty-nine in all) with two large television rooms at one end, the TV's are placed on shelves with about twelve to fifteen chairs in front of each. Each landing has shower rooms with two showers and two 'association rooms': small, oddly shaped rooms where hair is dried, clothes are ironed and in which inmates sit when they're fed up with their cells. The Assistant Governor's and Chief Officer's offices are on the second landing alongside the 'canteen' where inmates are paid every week. The fourth landing consists of a few cells, the staff room, two nurses' offices and a dispensary, plus a sectioned-off annexe with the doctor's office and three cells, used for punishment or hospitalisation, depending on what category you come under. They are sometimes used for both, which is quite interesting logistically.

H Wing was cold, comfortless and claustrophobic with an

atmosphere of mild paranoia and intense security. The place is small: it only takes about ten minutes, if that, to look round it. Drab and desolate, cut off from the main prison, it was a prison within a prison, creating a sense of complete isolation from the outside world, and eventually came to be known as 'the submarine'. It was the first wing adapted specifically as a top-security wing for female inmates. Inmates are labelled 'Category A' and thus identified as a potential menace to society. In all the time I spent there, there were only ever ten Cat As altogether; the rest of the population was made up of lifers in for murder, arsonists, drug dealers, child abusers and a whole series of petty offenders.

The day I arrived there was no one around, I later learned that everyone had been locked in. This happened a few times in the future when any so-called 'infamous' prisoners arrived: everyone would be locked in, for what reason I never discovered as we would all meet eventually. However, it made no odds to me; I had been isolated for so long and by now was thoroughly used to my own company, so the thought of meeting others had no great appeal for me. My mental state was such that if I had been left locked in my cell for evermore, I don't think I would have objected. Objectively, I was beyond feeling or reason: I moved when they said move and never questioned or wondered where I was, or what was happening. It's very hard to describe such an emptiness of feeling. A draining of the soul, a state of total apathy and abjectness to the nth degree, where physically one functions but mentally one is totally indifferent. Whether I cut myself off deliberately is hard to say. I certainly never gave a thought to it, just lay in my cell and let everyone else decide my fate. That first day I saw no one. I heard people moving around the wing, echoing voices (a feature of H wing with its high roof) and footsteps passing the door. Later in the evening the Governor called, accompanied by his usual entourage of officers, and enquired if I was feeling all right. How do you tell someone you're not feeling at all? He informed me that I would be 'in association' the following day. This meant being out of my cell and mixing with other prisoners during work and recreation hours.

The next morning I was woken by the sound of ringing

bells around 7 a.m. These were the 'aggro' bells and were tested every morning: they were installed to be used whenever a troublesome situation arose, for example a fight that might get out of hand. A voice at the door calls, in case you are still asleep, accompanied by an anonymous eye peering through the spyhole checking you're out of bed. You're supposed to be washed, using the water you brought by plastic jug or bucket to your cell the previous night, dressed and have the bed made by the time the cell doors are opened around 7.50 a.m. Then 'slop out', a foul function: you carry your pot to the sluice to empty the contents and wash it out. The smell is disgusting and the whole process demoralising and degrading, for inmates and officers alike, a task you could never get used to if you were in prison for a hundred years.

One dubious privilege of existing in H Wing is that each inmate has her own cell, a rule applied to every top-security prison, whether male or female. But far from making me feel that this was the penal equivalent of the Ritz, I felt that the routines were like those of a hospital. Patients have to wake, eat and sleep at times suitable to the nursing staff. The night shift knocks off at dawn and breakfast is prepared by the next lot. The third shift want everyone nicely tucked in, good and early, so the night people only have to sit a vigil, so to speak. I've never understood why the hours of these shifts can't be altered so that saner schedules can be given to staff and inmates alike, but perhaps that, in prison, is part of the punishment. The rigid routine of undeviating times for eating, sleeping and working is also I think a contributory factor to institutionalisation. How can one later slip back into the hours that society considers normal when one has spent a good piece of one's life totally out of sync with the rest of the country?

For a long time I didn't mix very well. I didn't really want to know who these people were or what they were in for; I didn't want to talk to them, so I was judged 'weird'. My weight had dropped a stone over the months on remand and trial; as I was only seven and a half stone to begin with, the loss of so much body weight made me quite skeletal. My moods swung wildly and I didn't converse much. I kept to myself, worked when I had to, slept when I didn't. I wasn't bothered whether people liked me or not, whether they spoke or not; my relationship with others was merely one of silent physical presence. I worked and ate alongside them, now and again speaking, but the interest factor was nil. These days such behaviour is recognised as stress reaction; in the early 1970s, however, it wasn't recognised at all. Psychiatrists were reserved for the obviously mentally ill. A woman convicted of a violent and heinous offence was viewed as bad and not as mad. With aid and, perhaps, medication I'm sure I would not have had to go through all the emotional disturbance I experienced. Not realising that I was ill, I certainly didn't ask for any treatment. In retrospect, maybe this was a good thing: because of my low body weight many medications have an adverse effect on me. In later years I did occasionally ask for sleeping medication, which though helpful, was an aid I didn't really want to get hooked on.

Many years later in Holloway I met a woman who had been at Durham in those first couple of years and I had no recollection of them. They remembered me as 'different'. This difference was to set me apart all through those years, a difference made up of many factors. I was Category 'A', which meant being accompanied by two officers wherever I went. They carried a little book in which were written my movements and what time I went where. If I had to go to the dentist, which is in the male part of the prison, I was accompanied by a male dog-handler as well as two female staff; other inmates could go there with just one officer. I was subject to constant cell changes and strip searches, was not allowed to work in certain parts of the wing, and wasn't allowed to clean on the 'flat', as it was too near the main exit gate of the wing and the cleaners there had to clean outside the wing. The meals were prepared in the main part of the prison by male inmates and brought by trolley to the wing, on a rota basis. Two inmates were allotted the daily task of bringing this in from the outside doors; I was never placed on this list.

Anyone who wanted a visit had to be 'vetted' by Special Branch officers. I could only write to people I knew before I came into prison and those who were deemed 'suitable', which left me with three or four visitors and correspondents for at least the next ten years and thus no chance of building new relationships even if I had wanted to. Have you ever tried sustaining a family relationship for ten years based on a letter every two weeks and a visit every six months or so? I was constantly watched: even at night there was no relief, the light had to be left on for 'observation'. I complained bitterly about this, the nightlight wasn't dim enough to gain relief. Eventually I was told I could have the light left on or switched off. If off, I would still be subject to hourly checks, when the light would be flicked on. For a while I asked for the lights to be switched off, but as I was constantly awakened by the light being switched on and off throughout the night in the end I told them to leave it on. Years later, proper dimmed lighting was installed and although this was far more satisfactory, I was overjoyed when I was downgraded from Cat A and was allowed to sleep with no light on.

Being Cat A also meant that you were in some way 'political'. The probation service has quite an important role in the prison system: its job is to help inmates keep in contact with their families, and to provide help and advice in whatever ways they can. Usually an inmate has a probation officer allocated from their home town and this person visits regularly, helps the inmate secure a job, and writes reports on the inmate for such things as parole reviews. There are also probation officers who work expressly in prisons and deal with day-to-day problems. Because I hadn't really lived permanently in England since leaving school, I didn't have a 'home town' probation officer. This didn't bother me at all, as I regarded them as less than able to help most inmates; most of them succeeded only in creating more problems. Many were out of touch with what was happening in the prisons and most inmates regarded them as part of the establishment. I'm happy to say that the probation service seems to have improved over the years. But their attitude to those regarded as 'politicals' was less than helpful. I was told by one probation officer that they had decided not to get involved with the 'political' inmates as they felt we were beyond help, our 'politics' ensuring that there would be no point in the probation service trying to encourage us to 'change our ways'. So we were given no advice about rehabilitation. They had passed judgment and washed their hands, without enquiring of any of the 'politicals' whether this was really the case.

I suffered enormously from the deprivation of liberty: being constrained within a fixed space was and is the greatest punishment I could imagine. I love to travel, to meet new people and to go for a walk whenever I feel like it. I had mostly worked outdoors or in jobs which were not on a routine nine-to-five basis, so to be locked within walls year after year, looking at the same faces and following a boring routine, made me feel like screaming with frustration at times: I even felt physically sick at the thought that I might spend the rest of my life in this manner. Since my release I have walked such distances that my feet began to blister, and have loved every minute of it!

I thought of these and many other issues when, at 8 p.m., it was back to my little box for another night's bang-up, to think and, perhaps, dream, yet I daydreamed rather more. I had often watched films on TV and revelled in the beautiful scenery; later, I would rerun the scenes in my mind and sometimes I cried and wished I was there. I thought of escape (which many inmates think of at some stage in their sentence) and spent hours making plans in my head. They came to nothing; I knew as I made them they would come to nothing. H Wing is forbidding in its security: we used to say a mouse might get in, but it would never get out! I never dreamed of revenge or retribution on those who had brought me to this situation; usually I just thought that one day when I was out I might meet them and then I would just say, 'Why? What have you got out of all this?' Many inmates dreamed about having a nice home, maybe a country cottage, with loving husband and kids. They knew they would probably never achieve this idyllic lifestyle, but it helped them to escape the dull monotony and greyness. I never thought about this: I wanted to travel, to meet new people and to see new countries, to be able to do whatever I wanted when I wanted, to eat tasty and pleasant food. There were times when I felt an instant depression on thinking such thoughts.

Despite the fact that Durham was my 'home' for fifteen years, I never regarded it as such and never became attached to my cell, although we were all allowed to furnish our cells with brightly coloured bedspreads, curtains and rugs, all of which had to be applied for. 'Applications' means you have to go to the office and ask the officer for things, for example if you want someone to bring in books on a visit. All applications are written down in a book which is taken out on the day of your visit to check that any item brought in has been applied for; if not, your visitors have to take it back home with them. Expected parcels also have to be applied for. My French friend, Anne Yvonne, sent me a yellow-patterned bedspread and beige rug to cover the lino tiles on the floor, and my mum sent me curtains, with wire and hooks (prisoners had to put these up themselves: the only problem was the stone walls, so we screwed the hooks into the frame of the window). We could put photos up on the cork boards. I did this at first, but stopped after a while. Cat A prisoners were subjected to regular cell changes, so every few weeks we had to pack all our things and move to another cell, for reasons of security, just in case we had started digging out of the cell – some hope, with those walls! Pinning up and taking down photos every few weeks made them very tatty, so in the end I didn't bother and stuck posters up instead. We weren't allowed to stick anything on the walls, again for security reasons. It all sounded very illogical to me, even more so when I found out that any foodstuffs sold in glass containers were not allowed because of the risk of people smashing the glass and mutilating themselves or others. The fact that we had glass windows and glass mirrors and stuck up our posters and photos with drawing pins and needles wasn't considered a risk.

There was a small library, converted from a cell, which didn't hold many books, although someone from the public library would bring books every few months. We were allowed as many educational books as needed in our cells, but only six of any other type, such as novels. Radios and record-players were allowed, but for many years only radios without an FM band, because FM was said to interfere with police and prison officers' radios – maybe they were worried we would hear some secrets. No ornaments or knick-knacks were permitted.

Female inmates are allowed to wear their own clothes, although we were restricted to four sets each in our cells. Any other clothing was stored in 'property'. We could change sets once a month if we liked, but many inmates didn't even have four sets to their name. A clothing grant of £140 was allotted to each inmate on entry into prison, but if you already had enough money you wouldn't get this; it was mainly given to inmates who didn't have family or visitors, or those whose families didn't have sufficient funds to buy clothes. When the clothes began to wear out you could ask for replacements, or ask your visitors to bring some in for you. All washing of clothes was done in a large industrial machine in the workroom by an inmate; if you wanted your sweaters to stay the same size and shape you washed them yourself.

Every Saturday we would be given an issue of washing powder, a sachet of shampoo, a bar of White Windsor soap (imprinted with the Queen's head, and only good for washing the floor), Tampax or STs and about seven tissues, which had to last a week. Tissues were much coveted in prison. Not only were they good for snotty noses, they were used for removing make-up and in place of the toilet paper, which was shiny on one side and always scratched your bum. Later on, we were allowed to buy boxes of them with our private spending money and then the authority began to issue a box a week. Such was the luxury of having hundreds of tissues that we invented colds, just to use them.

Let's not forget that we earned money too. There were only two types of work available. One was as a wing-cleaner, the prison Mrs Mopp. The job was to clean all sluice areas, shower rooms, washrooms and association rooms, and scrub the landing and the stairs. This was supposed to take all day. In the years to come, I became very adept and quick at this work and usually finished around dinner, as the lunch hour was always termed. Then I had to find somewhere to hide for the rest of the day from the staff, who thought finishing early meant you hadn't done it properly. But initially I was sent to the workroom, where I was placed at a sewing machine and given slips of material to practise on. Eventually I was given the task of machining hems on towels and making dark blue dungarees for the male inmates and our own cleaners (I learned a lot about the *haute couture* of Maison Durham). Our wages were around 58p per week. Just think what you could do with all that. In 1974 it bought half an ounce of tobacco, matches, papers and perhaps a packet of teabags. By the time I left prison my wage had risen to £4.90 a week – there's inflation for you. Items such as tobacco could be purchased once a week from the prison canteen, where we could also buy soft drinks, crisps, sweets, coffee, sugar, stamps and batteries for radios.

Each inmate was allowed what is termed 'private spends': money sent in by family or friends, if they could afford it, and kept for the inmate in the administration offices. Once a month you could spend a certain amount (but no more than around £230 a year) on items such as cosmetics, toiletries or batteries (no smoking requisites or foodstuffs were allowed). This was all well and good for those inmates with money, but I felt quite sorry for the poor sods who couldn't have even this small privilege to make their lives a little more dignified and independent. In prison there's constant worry and nit-picking over money: even the cost of a single stamp can be viewed in terms of bankruptcy. I've talked about money, whereas in actual fact we never handled it. Wages were, and still are, paid out on paper. Each week you're given a slip of paper with the amount earned written on the top. You write down what you want to buy, and on canteen day you're given your goods and sign to state you've received them. Any change is added to the following week's slip. Similarly with private spends: once a month you get the slip of paper with the amount you have 'banked' for you, write your list of requirements, the officer goes into the town and buys it, you then sign for the amount spent and the change is banked for the following month. For a while in Durham we were given real money as our wages, but this was stopped. The change to paper helped reinforce institutionalisation. It was said that it was to stop inmates from threatening others into handing the money over and bartering, but as this went on anyway with other items such as cosmetics and tobacco, I couldn't see the point. Bartering itself was not disapproved of; it was more the fear that an inmate would become a 'baron' and gain profit from other inmates. Apparently this practice is well known in male prisons but there was little evidence of it in the female system.

In eighteen years' imprisonment I must have spent at least 150,000 hours alone, which is more time in total solitude than most people spend in a lifetime. This figure is calculated on being locked up for the night from 8 p.m. to 8 a.m. and does not include hours spent locked up because of staff shortages or lock-up during the day for one reason or another. The view from my window was rather uninspiring, even if I'd cared to clamber on to the bedrail to look out. I could see the perimeter fence surrounding the wing and, directly opposite, a wing housing male inmates. This wouldn't have mattered if my solitude had been chosen; enforced privacy is very different. Everyone viewed the lock-up period differently: some women would shout conversations to the men opposite through their windows, some would read or listen to the radio, some would cry and some would pace up and down hating every minute, craving the company of another human being. Some would mutilate themselves with whatever came to hand, and there were also a few who found their own thoughts too hard to bear and killed themselves. Having been in solitude for 23 out of 24 hours a day in Risley, the idea of being locked up every night for twelve hours in H Wing was no great hardship, since I was out mixing with others during the day. Being a bit of a loner, I never really minded being locked up; it became a period of rest from the chaotic lifestyle of the prison. Mixing with sometimes volatile inmates all day and coping with the tension and stress of even a 'normal' daily routine, I was glad to escape to a place where I could breathe slowly for a while. There were, of course, physical disadvantages – there's nothing worse than being locked in a cell in which there is no toilet, worst of all when your period begins. There were times when a period would start in the middle of the night and there was no water to wash yourself, no STs or Tampax to hand, and no chance of an officer unlocking the door to give you some. The feeling of degradation was great. I quickly got into the habit of ensuring I always had sanitary protection stashed in my cell.

There were also times when I couldn't sleep, which brought me to the edge of a raging frustration. If I was outside, I would have made a hot drink, gone for a walk, watched TV or read a book. But here all I could do was prowl the length of the cell, hoping I would tire myself sufficiently to sleep. Thank God, these times were few and far between, and after reading for a couple of hours I would usually sleep easily for the rest of the night.

I'd been in H Wing for about eighteen months and during that time my attitude had been one of distance. I communicated little and never got involved in any confrontations, projecting a position of 'Don't bother me and I won't bother you.' Staff who knew me during this period told me they thought I was a 'snotty little bastard' because I didn't speak much and if I did my tone implied, 'Piss off, I really don't want to talk to you.' Little did they know I would have loved to talk to someone, sit down and have a good heart-to-heart, but I was afraid: afraid they would write it all down and the whole thing would start up again in another, even more menacing way. I just didn't trust anyone. Now and again I would be 'summoned' to the wing governor's office for a discussion on 'how I was settling in'. I would be panic-stricken during these 'discussions', seeing them more as 'interrogations' – why else would they want to talk to me? I went on the defensive, became stroppy and retaliated with silly phrases like, 'Well, you've got me now, so what else do you want', not realising that I was reinforcing the idea in people's heads that I was guilty. So great was my inner turmoil and confusion that I often questioned myself when I was banged-up at night, staring at myself in the mirror, wondering who I was and did I do it or not.

'Can I remember doing it?' 'No.' 'Then I can't have done it.' 'Ah,' said a voice in my head, 'but you can't remember much of remand or the trial, so maybe you can't remember doing it.' 'If you didn't do it, what are you doing here?'

The answer to that was easy: I hadn't a clue and didn't want to work it out. Looking back and questioning was too hard a reality for me then. I ignored the fact that I might be in this situation for the rest of my life and that no one really gave a damn. Everyone here was perceived as guilty and to say 'innocent' was to bring scorn, derision and disbelief on oneself. I wasn't strong enough, mentally, to handle the situation and accepted, however unhappily, that I could hide in the anonymity of a prison number.

However, it all caught up with me one sunny day. It was dinner time. I was sitting at my usual place picking at the usual mess of a meal. I happened to look up and glance around the wing and it suddenly felt like I'd been dealt a blow on the head with a large blunt instrument. I was struck with a horrible and certain clarity of awareness that I would probably be sitting at this same table, looking at the same view, doing the same work, eating this same meal, on the same day, the following week, and all the weeks, months and years to come. There would be no holidays in the sun, no boyfriends, no marriage, no kids, no popping out to the shops for a paper, no walks in the park, no flowers or trees, no paddles in the sea, no train or bus rides – just sameness. Unlock 7.45 a.m., slop out, breakfast, work, dinner, exercise, work, tea, telly, supper, bang-up 8 p.m. A walking time-table, totally and perfectly primed to perform certain functions at certain times without deviation. The food became sawdust in my mouth and my mind began to slide into claustrophobic and suffocating cotton wool, not white, but black, thick and noxious. The next few weeks were a nightmare, I struggled through the days, surly, rude and offensive.

'What the fuck are you looking at?'

'Nothing, Judy.'

'Well, piss off, then.'

'What the fuck do you call this? Food? Bollocks!'

I refuse to eat for days and am hospitalised. I lie in a dreary cell which smells stale and unused; it suits me. At nights I crouch under the blanket, head covered, praying, 'Let me not wake up in the morning.' The morning comes with a bright sun, mocking at my misery, a bird perches on the windowsill and sings, I scream, 'Get away, you bastard.' My legs ache, my body screams for food whilst my mind screams for oblivion. I take a cigarette from my stash outside the window. 'You're not allowed to smoke if you're not eating,' says the nasty doctor with nasty ideas. I puff my fag contentedly, my head aches and I feel slightly sick, my heart thumps loudly in my chest, warning me that fags and no food is not a healthy combination. Good, maybe I'll get a heart attack. I want to pee, but feel too weak to move. I won't talk to people, won't get up, I cry in furious rage, 'I don't want to be here any more! I want to die.' I hate this place, I hate everyone, I hate myself even more.

So it went on, until one morning I woke up and thought to myself, 'What an arsehole you are, Ward, lying there feeling sorry for yourself.' The cotton wool began to thin and I began to feel better and stronger. Not immediately and completely. In the years to come I would suffer more periods of depression and dive into them unable to function, but none would ever be as strong and lasting as that first period. I would also at times be subject to what I can only describe as an immediate and intense feeling of melancholy. For instance, one evening, I was talking to one of the nursing sisters as she prepared medications. The dispensary was on the top landing where there was a marvellous view of Durham Cathedral. As we talked, I moved over to look out of the window. It was summertime, the sky was full of red and gold, with flecks of purple in the distance; the sun was setting behind the cathedral. I looked at this for a moment and felt as if I was dying on the spot. Tears formed in my eyes and I cried, for what, for whom and for why, I had no idea. I just felt a great and painful ache in my heart, as if someone or something had died. The sister was great and tried to cheer me up, but I've never forgotten that moment. Over the years I began to realise that everyone has a reason for living, for going on, in even the most daunting of circumstances and that living and going on is a reason in itself.

7

Durham 1976–84

Even so it was very hard for me to appreciate the reason for working in the workshop. Most prison regimes try to ensure that inmates spend as much time as possible out of their cells. One of the ways they do this is to set up a workshop. I found the workshop not in the least stimulating and became increasingly bored and frustrated having to spend my time machining overalls, towels and other items destined for inmates' use. As the months passed I tried to find reasons for spending time out of the workshop, without much success. But in 1976 I discovered that one could have up to ten hours out of the workshop every week for educational purposes, and I decided to enrol on an Open University course. I soon began to enjoy and take a deep interest in my studies. The first course was an Arts Foundation Course, which was an introduction to the OU courses available in the arts section. I had to write an assignment every six weeks or so on various subjects, ranging from art and architecture to philosophy and history. I found the self-discipline of studying more or less by correspondence and alone very difficult at first, but soon discovered I was quite able to switch off and absorb myself in reading. It proved to be a real form of 'escape' from my surroundings. The only slight problem was that I had no one with whom I could discuss what I was studying.

There were tutors for the OU courses, but they only came in about once every six weeks. I had always had interesting conversations with the nursing staff, who I viewed at one remove from the staff on the wing. I soon found that they liked to discuss the courses and we talked about my assignments at length and with a vigour which any professor would have found fascinating. I also attended evening classes run by teachers who usually taught in schools by day and offered courses, some up to O-level standard, in English, Spanish and maths. Class hours were from 5.30 to 7.30 p.m., with only six or seven inmates allowed in each class. This ratio of inmates to teacher was due to the smallness of the 'class-rooms', which were actually our usual association rooms. Although we benefited in being given more attention due to the small numbers, other inmates had nowhere to associate when classes were running and were restricted to their cells or the TV rooms.

I attended Spanish, art and English classes and particularly enjoyed art. During the evening bang-up and at weekends I spent many hours producing artwork of various kinds, mostly figurative and landscapes, using watercolours, charcoal, pencil or pen and ink. Although the work was of no great value or merit, the concentration and the results left me in a pleasant and satisfied state of mind. I like the company of others, but I value my own physical and mental 'space'. Since my release I have lived on my own, enjoying the company of friends and relatives who stay with me from time to time. Even now I suppose, I can take or leave company. Having spent eighteen years in enforced company with sometimes volatile and violent inmates, being by myself is a luxury I enjoy.

Around this time Carole Robinson and Anne Maguire arrived on the wing. Carole, one of the Guildford four, released on appeal in 1989, was sentenced to life for the Guildford pub bombings when she was eighteen years old. I was amazed that anyone could think that this young girl had taken part in any terrorist action. On the outside, she had taken drugs and was generally a layabout, sleeping rough at times. In prison she took drugs prescribed by the doctor and was widely regarded as a hypochondriac. Who wouldn't be after being convicted of such an offence when she was totally innocent? Anne Maguire had been sentenced to fourteen years for supposedly maintaining a 'bomb factory' in her home. There were seven convicted in all in her case, including her husband, two sons, one aged just thirteen at the time, a brother-in-law, a friend and Giuseppe Conlon, who died some years later in prison of TB. He was the father of Gerry Conlon, also one of the Guildford four.

Our relationship was ambivalent and although we talked over our cases and instantly recognised each other as innocent, we didn't group together. Each preferred to get through her sentence as well as she could, while recognising that we would support each other if need be. Also in H Wing at that time were the Gillespie sisters who had been sentenced to fourteen years for fire-bombing. Although they have never publicly claimed their innocence, it has been regarded in many circles that there was something distinctly 'iffy' about their case. Anne was the most vociferous of us all regarding her innocence: she told anyone and everyone who would listen to her, but not many did. At the time I didn't protest too much, for many reasons.

The most important was a fear that my family would again suffer unwarranted publicity and hostility as they had in 1974, and I was very anxious to protect them, as I still am today. There were no support groups at that time and from watching the result of Anne's protestations, which achieved little apart from turning her into a nervous wreck, I knew that I would be wasting my time shouting in deaf ears. Anne and Carole were waiting for their appeals to be heard; I did not have even that small satisfaction.

After being sentenced, I was advised by my barrister that it would not be wise to appeal at that time. There was a small but widespread bombing campaign in London, and the Guildford bombing had occurred during my trial. Knowing little of the law, and in a disturbed state, an appeal was something of which I was entirely ignorant. I was not informed, in a way that I understood anyway, of one small, but important, point regarding appeals. One has a period of twenty-eight days, after sentencing, in which to give notice and lodge information of any future appeal. It wasn't until about eighteen months later that I discovered this, so any hope of appeal was lost before it had begun. I was absolutely furious and this information contributed to my lack of confidence and probably my decline into what I term as my 'Great Depression'. Any hope of appeal would have to be based on the generosity of the Home Secretary in referring my case to the Court of Appeal, supported by the producing of new evidence. There was plenty of this at the time, but neither myself nor anyone else was aware that it was available.

There was also the issue of Cat A status. I wasn't allowed to write to people I didn't know before being sentenced, so any attempt to write to an MP, other than my constituency one, or to people who might have taken an interest, was not allowed. I turned my attention to trying to get through day-to-day living on H Wing. It wasn't until Anne was released some nine years later that interest in my case slowly began to grow and support groups and media pressure formed a voice of opinion, mainly due to people like Anne, who spoke out constantly and finally forced people to take notice.

Some time in the early 1980s Peter Hodgkinson appeared on the wing. On first seeing this man, I had no idea who he was. A friend told me he was a probation officer, probably the best probation officer she'd ever encountered. Intrigued by this description of someone who worked for a service which is not, generally, held in high esteem, I determined to meet this paragon. After he had visited the women he had as clients, I asked if I could speak to him. At first we were both pretty cagey, speaking on mundane matters. The more I listened to him, the more I realised that this man was not one of the usual type. He had studied criminology and sociology intensively, travelling abroad to gain experience and insight. From then on, Peter visited me whenever he came to H Wing. As a probation officer, there wasn't much he could do for me, as a friend and mentor he was invaluable. Until I met Peter, I had no one to project my thoughts, moans and groans on to and he became my 'whipping boy'. Through letters and visits I was able to unleash my fears and hopes about my situation in a way I would never have done with my parents for fear of distressing them. I knew that Peter could take it all in his stride and with his witty sense of humour and unfailing logic he guided me through the ups and downs of prison life. Some years later, he left the probation service to become a senior lecturer in law and I was sorry to see him go. Fortunately, since my release, I have been in touch with him. As well as lecturing he is also the chairman of 'Deathwatch', a single-issue human rights organisation campaigning for the abolition of capital punishment world-wide. I too supported this group, mindful of the fact that if the death penalty had not been abolished in Britain I would not be writing this book.

In Peter's place came Angela, a woman around the same age as myself, and holding, luckily, more or less the same views as Peter. We became good friends and she was greatly supportive in the months up to my appeal.

People have asked me where and how my family figured in my life, especially in the early years at Durham. Except for regular visits from my mother and stepfather and a couple of visits from my sisters, the truth is they were not very supportive. As I understand their reasons, I am not particularly critical or judgmental. My parents were bewildered and frightened by what had happened to me. Scared of the police and seemingly surrounded by hostility in the media, they were unable to assess what their neighbours or friends might think or how they might react, and so retreated into a shell, from which they have now emerged, having lived in semi-fear and emotional distress for eighteen years. Having been brought up in an age when the police, the boss, the doctor, the magistrate and the MP were all regarded as awesome and omnipotent figures, they were totally ignorant of the procedure by which they could help me. There were no outspoken campaigners in the 1970s; no one was listening. We were not a close or articulate family. They were overwhelmed and afraid of the unfolding events and had neither the confidence nor the means to challenge decisions; they were simply unable to supply the kind of aggressive fight that might have helped.

There were other pressures too. In the early 1970s the police were still seen by most members of the public as benign Dixons and, as the political troubles in Northern Ireland escalated, Irish people were perceived as a violent and dangerous disruptive group. All my parents knew was that I had chosen to live there, a sort of rejection, I suppose, of my own community, and I had never taken much trouble to maintain links with my brothers and sisters. I can't and don't blame them for being less than saintly, they just didn't have a clue.

My stepfather, Sam, had got a job in another town and so most of the family moved house, but perhaps they were also keen to get away from the knowing glances of neighbours and the implied association with what was, after conviction, seen as an act of treason. In the small and small-minded community where she lived it would have been very difficult for Mum to face the shopkeepers and neighbours. The journalists and the police had fed them a pack of lies about me and they didn't really know what to do or how to be supportive, no-one had taught them how to cope with any even dimly comparable situation. Unfortunately, our family life had been constructed on a base of fragility, silences and illusions, not strength and acceptance, and this intensified after my sentence. Over the years my parents have learnt a little how to question, they have written numerous letters to the Home Office on my behalf and have become stronger. Now I feel a strong bond with my parents, yet there is still a long way to go with the rest of the family.

The visiting room in H Wing was very small. It held three or four tables, at one of which the staff sat throughout. As a Cat A, I was not allowed to have visitors when other inmates were having theirs. All visits had to be booked in advance to avoid too many people arriving on the same day. Visiting times were mornings and afternoons, any day of the week. I found the room inhibiting, as did my parents. We sat at a table, me on one side, them on the other, one officer at one end of the room and one opposite. Sometimes there were three officers. Any conversation was stilted; we were all conscious that two, maybe three, strangers were watching us and felt they were probably listening too. Although the majority of officers sat reading magazines and tried to be inconspicuous, the fact that they were in such close proximity was daunting. Our conversations mostly revolved around inanities on how they had got to Durham, what the weather was like and the cafés they had stopped at during their journey.

Other visitors came to H Wing: groups of trainee probation officers and policemen, or visiting magistrates. We resented the way they stared – curious, yet afraid to try and engage us in conversation. It was as if we were animals in the zoo, like those inmates of Bedlam who were treated like a freak show by the safely wealthy in the eighteenth century. Our reaction was either to ignore them or to put on a show and modify our behaviour especially for them. Who knows if the monkeys in the zoo scratch and squabble for their own benefit or because they know they are being used as entertainment? We would be deliberately moronic and even foul-mouthed: to us it was a game; they were our entertainment, not the other way round. This may sound as if we were supportive of each other, closing ranks against the perceived 'enemy'. On a very basic level there is a feeling of 'we're all in the same pit', but mostly friendships and alliances could change from day to day.

This is hardly surprising in a society like H Wing, a world within a world, limited by high walls with a constant under-current of personal tension. One day someone would be your closest confidante and the next you would be on oppo-site sides of a bitter row concerning some routine duty or other issue. The inmates, many of them obviously and understandably angry and frustrated, would create rows with the officers over things as petty as the amount of veget-ables on their plate compared to that given to another inmate. Boredom, a lack of trust and quality of life coupled with guilt and insecurity and a feeling that you are generally regarded as second-, if not third-class citizens, breeds a slight paranoia. A giggle means someone is laughing at you, a side-ways glance is perceived as challenging: your only choice is to challenge back, verbally or physically. Not to do so is to be regarded as a 'soft touch', a pushover, someone on whom the rest can work out their personal problems and frustra-tions, real or imagined. Anger, just like water, finds its own level and creates an escape route.

In the main I tried to avoid confrontations and in doing so played my own games. Many women resented an officer, especially a young one, telling them what to do. I adopted the practice of doing what they wanted before they asked, thus in a way gaining some slight power and control over my life and denying them the satisfaction of issuing an order. I would sometimes get locked in before the usual 8 p.m. bang-up, feeling that I was making a small choice and en-gaging in a little form of rebellion. It may seem no big thing to an outsider, but to me it was the beginning of gaining some form of independence. I soon discovered that in some ways the inmates themselves were contributing to their insti-tutionalisation. The evening association period was the time for filling flasks for the night and taking showers. It struck me that we were falling into the trap of doing these things at exactly the same time every night. After tea, around 5 p.m., many of the inmates would rush upstairs to shower and then downstairs to fill their flasks. I realised this was becoming a habit when one night I started to panic around 6 p.m. upon discovering I hadn't filled my flask. From then on, I deliberately avoided the 5 p.m. rush, sometimes forgetting to fill my flask altogether or not bothering to take a shower, religiously, every night. It afforded me a small feeling of decision.

Another way in which I asserted myself was never to call the Governor 'sir'. Addressing him in this way was seen as a sign of respect, but to my mind respect had to be earned and should be awarded to an individual one admired, not freely given just because he was in a position of power. Many governors passed through H Wing over the years; two or three years was the usual period of time before a governor moved on to a higher, or lower, position. I called them by their surname, if they were 'Jones', they were 'Jonesy'. It wasn't hard to discover their first names either and often I used them, prefixed by the word 'Uncle'. This astounded and embarrassed them, especially when they were showing visitors round and I would call out, 'Morning, Uncle Fred!' or whatever. I knew that by some I was regarded as cheeky and stroppy, but if I was going to suffer the indignity of patronising use of terms such as 'ladies' or 'girls', they would have to put up with it too. Little things, little things, but they helped to keep me sane and helped me to endure.

Many inmates, after some years into their sentence, often felt threatened by any changes in their routine, so much so that there was great complaining when a decision was made to reorganise the workshop, even though their quality of life would be enhanced. In making small changes, I acquired the ability to take the big ones in my stride, which in turn helped me to acquire a more positive outlook.

At times I was viewed by the other inmates as rather strange. Some had noticed that I never seemed to get told what to do by the officers and felt I was a bit too compliant. The fact that I sometimes asked to be locked in earlier than normal also perplexed them. I explained my ideas about power and control: it was a theory which many of them began to toy with, and sometimes it was quite funny to see a few of them asking the staff to lock them in before the actual bang-up time. Some inmates thought my views on officers odd, because I refused to subscribe to the general view that 'all screws were bastards'. Some were, undoubtedly. Some were bullies and got a kick out of bossing us around and picking up a very respectable wage for it. There were others who were just doing a job and tried to be fair in doing so. And there were others with whom I became friendly and who were supportive and helped me through the years as much as they could within the confines of their job. I couldn't see how the staff were to blame for my situation; having been scapegoated myself, I was not prepared to use the staff as such, as a few inmates did. Yet, their inability to view accurately what was important to an inmate, even though they may have worked in the job for years, was irritating to me and sometimes led to dispute.

For instance, one of the main issues surrounding prisons is that of staff shortages. In H Wing we suffered very little bang-up because of this problem, mainly because it is a top-security wing and the Home Office prefers such prisons to be well staffed. However, in the summer, staff obviously took holidays and at times there were not enough staff to man the evening shifts. Thus, we would be locked up from as early as 5 p.m. One night when staff were at a premium, an officer had volunteered to do (well-paid) overtime so we wouldn't be locked up. In explaining this to a group of us, she obviously felt we should thank her for the 'favour'. I refused to do so, stating that it didn't really matter to me whether I was banged-up in the big 'box', that is the wing, or in the little 'box', my cell, the whole point being that I was still banged-up and what's the difference? She took umbrage at this, as she couldn't see my point of view at all. In fact, I would have preferred to be out watching TV or whatever, but I hid my vulnerabilities so that the more malicious officers could not scratch at them.

One of the more serious vulnerabilities was the strip-search. H Wing has always employed strip-searching, under the guise of security, and every inmate went through the regular hell of it. I suppose they thought it helped to maintain the rule of law. Sometimes the search would be cursory, at other times ridiculously thorough, with every postcard scrutinised, hems and linings of clothes felt and non-existent secret hiding places peered for. I had, over the years become used to this and like most other inmates usually read a book or ignored the whole proceedings. Sometimes I would talk to the officers doing the search as some made it quite obvious they didn't like what they were doing. Most of us got a bucket of water and scrubbed down our cell after these searches, a result of feeling that our privacy has been invaded, a stranger had touched our personal possessions. I can understand how people who have been burgled often feel they want to move house.

One one occasion, I completely lost my rag. The younger of the two officers doing the search was going through my clothes, amongst them some freshly laundered and ironed blouses. One by one she chucked the blouses on top of my cupboard as she checked them. I told her I wasn't having this and she should either fold them up or put them back on the hangers. She said it wasn't her job to do that. I replied that it was my job to punch her face in if she didn't. The older pressed a warning hand on my shoulder; the younger sneered that I would be severely punished if I touched her. I told her it would be well worth it: I meant it, and was well prepared to lay one on her. The older officer intervened and told her to put the clothes back on the hangers. This is how prison affects you. I must have had hundreds of searches, yet that was one that annoyed me most intensely. It wasn't the fact that my clothes were creased, it was a more a recognition of being diminished in some way.

It is the most degrading thing to have to strip off in front of complete strangers and is probably the closest thing to rape that many inmates have to endure. I hated it and often thought that I would refuse to strip but the consequences of such refusal would have been either a spell in punishment and/or a forced strip-search, in which the officers would take off your clothes for you. I decided to take the course of not caring. I would stroll blithely into the cell and take off my clothes, all the time telling myself that it was no big deal. In the end I think I really didn't care. I had played the game of 'who cares' for so long, it became part of my attitude to prison and I applied it to all sorts of situations. In doing so I became mentally stronger, to such a degree that I gave up worrying about the everyday, petty issues and wrangles, realising that I didn't need to totally immerse myself in the prison culture to survive.

I could see no point in mindlessly fighting things that were beyond my power to change. Equally I was aware that there was no point in being Miss Nice. Like all Cat A inmates I knew that my behaviour, good or bad, wouldn't count towards anything. The Home Office would review Cat As once a year to decide whether they should be downgraded to a lesser category, and in my case any such review would be judged in a political light. Any idea of cow-like obedience just didn't exist; it wouldn't get me out any sooner. If I was really annoyed about something, I realised quite early on, it was better to approach the highest authority, the Governor or the Home Office. Officers were powerless to resolve grievances. Apart from this, one of the problems of being a Cat A inmate was the officers' view that I wasn't really an 'ordinary' prisoner, so they left me and my problems to their superiors. It was just as well that I recognised this point of view and knew that in the main I was without even the basic aid given to the ordinary inmate. Over the years I appealed less and less to the staff in H Wing as it became apparent that those in the Home Office were also at a loss to provide any substantial support. The following quote taken from a letter sent to me by a Home Office bod in 1989 accurately sums up not only my situation but the faults in the system as a whole: 'When the system is faced by an unusual situation, if I may be allowed to describe you in these terms, it has very little to give on a personal level . . . the person who needs most help . . . is actually required to give more help in order to receive it. I don't know the way out of this impasse'. This was an answer to a letter I had written regarding a transfer to another prison after being decategorised. I have often wondered since whether the writer of this letter was aware that his colleagues had already undertaken three secret reviews of my case by then, a fact which was to be revealed years later at my appeal. Perhaps his awareness is reflected in his very candid and honest yet uncomfortable reply.

Over the years I had quite a lot of contact with the Home Office. If an inmate felt that the prison authorities were unable to give a satisfactory reply to whatever question one put to them, then one could appeal to the H. O. through a petition. The petition comprised an A4 lined sheet of prison-headed paper bearing the peculiar sentence, 'DO NOT WRITE BETWEEN THE LINES'. Maybe they hoped it would confuse enough inmates to make them give up any idea of petitioning. I had petitioned the H. O. numerous times on matters to do with conditions on the wing and, in particular, about my wish to be downgraded so I could move out of H Wing. Their replies were always very formal and stilted and usually 'no'. One day, feeling particularly frustrated at having been in H Wing for over twelve years, I decided to test their mettle again. I wrote saying that as H Wing had nothing left to offer me in the way of facilities I would like to be transferred. As I was Cat A and there were no other Cat A female wings in England, I had come up with a solution. I had heard that Rudolf Hess was in Spandau. He must surely be Cat A as he had the whole prison to himself so what about transferring me there? I would, of course, be very well guarded and would be able to keep Rudolf company in his loneliness. I sent the petition off not really expecting an answer. A couple of months later a reply came back. 'The Home Secretary has carefully and sympathetically considered your petition. However he is unable to transfer you to Spandau as you are not a German citizen.' Was *One Flew Over the Cuckoo's Nest* filmed in the Home Office I asked myself?

My attitude was considered by some of the staff to be unco-operative, and to a certain extent they were right. With the sentence I was serving, the threat of delayed parole for bad behaviour had no hold over me, but my stroppiness was mostly an attempt to impose my individuality on a lifestyle where such an idea was secondary to that of the mindless obedience much favoured in prisons. It was a difficult coexistence – with the officers, my fellow inmates and myself – and I tried to use the system to get what I could grab from it. One of the ways in which I asserted myself was by refusing to work, a major sin in prison. This wasn't because I was lazy: the work wasn't exciting but it certainly helped pass long, dull hours. I would sometimes point out the fact that it was 'my day off'. People outside had days off and even though we were off work at weekends, we never experienced a 'day off' from prison. If I refused to work, I would be left in my cell until the following day, thus getting my 'day off', until the morning of the following day when a report would be served on me and I would appear before one of the Governors for 'adjudication'.

An 'adjudication' is somewhat akin to a court session, only in smaller terms. The Governor is seated behind a desk or table, accompanied by a male 'bodyguard'. Also present are the Chief Officer and the officer who reported you, who will read out the evidence. Other officers may be there, if they think you're inclined to be violent and may jump over the table to give the Governor a smack on the nose. You are escorted in by an officer on each side, to stand before the Governor. The officers then turn and face you, hemming you in a small gap between their shoulders. Nowadays, everyone sits on chairs in an effort to make adjudications less intimidating. The Governor reads out the charge, then the officer reads out the 'evidence', what you did, when, and so on. You're asked whether you plead 'Guilty' or 'Not guilty' to the charge and are allowed to put forward any explanation, if you want to. The Chief Officer is asked for a summary of your past behaviour and any other offences, after which the Governor gives his decision. Few inmates are found 'Not guilty'. Punishment is then 'awarded': this could be loss of wages, private spends, association or remission (loss of time off for good behaviour), a caution or a suspended sentence, dependent on subsequent good behaviour for a period of time. As a lifer I couldn't lose remission and for refusing to work the usual punishment was loss of wages and/or loss of private spends for an amount of time stipulated by the Governor. With very serious charges, usually violence, the Governor can remand an inmate, meaning confine them to their cells (house arrest), until such time as they appear before the Board of Visitors for adjudication. This board is made up of magistrates, and is deemed to be an independent body. Called in to adjudicate on serious offences, it can give heavier punishments than those which a Governor is allowed to 'award'.

The board members also visit on a regular individual basis and an inmate may approach them with a complaint which has not been satisfactorily resolved by the prison authorities. If, for instance, you have a complaint about the Chief Officer, you explain to the board member, who then goes to the Chief Officer and asks what he or she should do. It's unfortunate that board members know little of the day-to-day running of a prison and even less of inmates' needs and wants. Many of them are imbued with Victorian ethics such as 'Cleanliness is next to Godliness'; they often walk around the prison uttering inanities like, 'Isn't machining very interesting work?' or, 'I heard you got a pay rise of 5p, absolutely splendid!' If they hear someone laughing, they think they're having a great time – the probability that it's a sign of hysteria wouldn't occur to them. I may be a little harsh on them, but in the view of most inmates they are a punitive body and little else. The inmates' awareness that a complaint against a member of staff may bring reprisal, coupled with the knowledge that the staff have the power and control to 'get their own back', often prevents any complaint being lodged in writing or brought to the attention of the Board of Visitors. They are regarded as too 'establishment', rather like the many 'do-gooders' who seem attracted to prisons.

'Prison visitors' come under the label 'do-gooders'. These are members of the public who are often connected to a religious group. Having been approved by the Home Office, they are allowed access to the 'inner sanctum' of the prison area, including inmates' cells. Their aim is to offer moral support and advice and establish a friendly relationship. To their credit, they are prepared to give up their free time and volunteer to visit inmates, with a sincere wish to help. However, many of them feel they must convey their own religious views on the inmates in such a way that it appears patronising. They have little or no knowledge of how a prison is run and no conception of what it is like for an inmate, so they are of little use in resolving the many problems that beset individuals. Many of them are seen as far more than a little voyeuristic and more concerned that they are 'doing good' to themselves rather than the inmates. Some of these prison visitors are quite well-known figures, for instance Lord Longford. Many years ago I met Lord Longford when he was visiting H Wing and, though there is no doubting his sincerity and commitment, I find it strange that he only appears to concern himself with 'high-profile' inmates when there are many others who would benefit from his power and authority. Fortunately, it is not compulsory to have visits from these people and I, along with many other inmates, had little to do with them.

Over the years I spent many days locked up on punishment and lost quite an amount of my wages. Having adapted a 'you can't get to me' attitude, I didn't resent the punishment, more the fact that asserting individuality was viewed as a punishable offence. Most of my 'adjudications' were conducted, on my part, in a jocular manner, in an effort to impose my view of what a farce the whole system is. A farce in that, either wittingly or unwittingly, the system institutionalises a person, degrades and demoralises the ego, inadvertently taking away what little sense of pride and dignity an inmate may have, all in the name of rehabilitation. It punishes those who try to say, 'Here I am, an individual with personality and a character and this is my way of trying to retain that individuality.' It's unfortunate that punishment, and the inmates' fear of it, is used as a major form of control in the prison system, with any form of initiative being viewed as a threat.

Many inmates endeavoured to assert their individuality through personal hygiene and appearance. Ninety-nine per cent of female prisoners take pride in their appearance, which challenges the widely held view that most women only do so for the benefit of men. Those who would have worn make-up outside would continue to do so inside. Those who plucked their eyebrows and shaved their legs would carry on these habits. It's a sort of barometer of pride, self-esteem, a fight, almost, against the degradation of such things as slopping out. With our private cash, once a month we were allowed to buy cosmetics. An officer would be given the job of purchasing them from shops in the town, which made it difficult in terms of choice and range as we had to write what we wanted on a list and hope for the best. However, most of the time we got what we had asked for. There was also a 'beauty' class, where inmates were informed about different types of cosmetics and learned how to apply them. Later on, hairdressing classes were introduced, but for a good many years we had to rely on an amateur hairdresser, amongst the inmates or sometimes the staff, and many's the weird cut they produced, I can tell you. When proper classes and teachers were introduced, some inmates became very proficient.

There were women, who because of mental illness or depression caused by their situation, didn't make any effort even to look tidy. Some of them smelt terribly, a great aroma of staleness and sweat accompanying them wherever they walked. The reaction to these women was varied. If it was realised they were 'not the full shilling', they would be gently cajoled by staff and inmates alike into the shower and encouraged to wash their clothes and hair. If it was thought there was no reason for such tardiness, pointed remarks and sometimes downright rudeness would be employed such as, 'Cor, you stink. Go and get in the shower, you dirty sod.' One woman, who came from an upper middle-class background and had taught at university, was ordered into the showers by the staff each morning, until she began to look after herself and her clothes. Women usually pay more attention to hygiene than men, and this was reflected not only in their appearance but also in the way the wing was cleaned to a high standard. Each inmate was responsible for keeping her cell clean. Most of us did so, but some did not. At one time, a few officers were deployed each morning to check that the cells were clean. They slipped into your cell, drawing a surreptitious finger across the top of the locker or wardrobe, glancing under the bed to check whether the potty was suffocating in the fluff which fell from the blankets. We dubbed them the 'Fluff Squad', and they were not taken seriously. The majority of us kept our cells pretty clean anyway.

Prison is a great place for observing others. I spent many hours just watching the other inmates and their reactions to their problems, difficulties and life in general. I became so interested in human nature that I wanted to study psychology, but in those days it was a forbidden subject – perhaps the authorities thought we just might apply it to them and find them lacking in some way. One aspect of psychology I learnt without being taught was that helping others was also helping oneself. As the years progressed and new inmates arrived, I realised I was viewed as someone who could help in various ways. The fact that I had done many years, was studying with the OU, knew my way around the rules extremely well and by now appeared to coexist with everyone on a more or less amicable level, was the initiative for many women to approach me for help and advice. I was unsure how to adopt this role of 'social-worker' at first, but as the years rolled by and I passed on what little advice and help I could, I saw that by helping others they, too, were also helping me to gain an inner strength and confidence. An awareness of self and dignity is most important to any inmate.

The use of prison argot is a psychological tool mainly employed by male inmates. Phrases such as 'doing your bird' and 'bang-up' help inmates relate to their surroundings and impose a more personal feeling on a very impersonal situation. I noticed that women do not use prison argot much, but many of the younger ones indulged in 'backslang'. This style of speech incorporates a vowel into words where a vowel is not required. The result sounds like gobbledegook and I'm afraid I have never mastered this art. Using backslang allowed inmates to talk in some privacy, as well as reducing somewhat the control and power of the staff and fostering amongst them a slight paranoia.

Myself and a friend, Lorna, a lifer some years younger than me, discovered that we could irritate the staff enormously using our own argot. As we are both from the Manchester area we often talked in local dialect using terms we were acquainted with. One of them was 'pobs'. Pobs, for the uninitiated, means a bowl of small pieces of bread and sugar covered with hot milk. I was often given this in my younger days to fill me up, as were many northern children. We found that the staff had no idea what 'pobs' were and we would incorporate the word into our sentences now and again. The result was amazing. Staff would ask us what it meant but we refused to tell them, delighting in our little power and their paranoia, which increased daily. We told the other inmates the meaning of the word and so began a period in which we would wind up the staff. We would walk round the wing and upon meeting another inmate, raise our fists and shout, 'Pobs!'. The staff began to get worried and irritable and even threatened us with punishment if we didn't stop doing this. We knew it wasn't a punishable offence and just laughed at them. It was quite an interesting insight into the psyche of some of the staff on H Wing. I thought it reflected how using such psychological ploys could reveal their insecurity at the thought of losing even some small control over the inmates.

When I speak of Durham in the 1970s and early 1980s it should be borne in mind that at that time Britain was still 'luxuriating' in the effects of a number of postwar reforms. People had enjoyed over thirty years of a decent health service, an excellent free education for those who were bright enough to grasp it and vast improvements in social and housing conditions. The climate was right, largely due to a succession of Labour governments (but partly because of the influence on ordinary people of these reforms), for the growth of greater public tolerance of previously unacceptable behaviour. Pacifism, for instance, was no longer a dirty word. Homosexuality had been legalised amongst consenting adults. Divorce was very much easier. Abortion, if not exactly on demand as its opponents claimed, had become an option. Most sexually active women used some form of contraception. All this would have been unthinkable twenty years earlier. Many of these changes, however, bypassed the prison service. It was as if many of those who ruled it and served in it were just as surely locked in outdated attitudes as we were locked inside our cells.

8

Durham 1984–86

By the early 1980s my relationship with some of the officers and nursing staff had progressed and strengthened. We spent many evening hours involved in games of trivial pursuit. Although I never discussed my case with the officers much, I did with the nursing staff, and two of them were very supportive and sent me letters of congratulations when the news of my appeal was announced. There were other officers that I despised and wouldn't pass the time of day with. They saw their role as one of power and authority and appeared to be lacking in even the basic psychological skills that some officers acquired after being in the job for a while. Many abused their power and showed an ignorance which made one wonder how they had got the job. They saw any inmate who had even a smattering of education as a threat and tried in little ways to undermine us, but only succeeded in revealing their own insecurities.

One officer would constantly pick upon and mimic an inmate who had a university degree and spoke with a 'posh' accent. She was continually upset at this and was at a loss how to respond. I told her she should give the officer a mouthful, using the longest words she could think of. So, one day, after receiving verbal from this officer, the inmate turned round and said, 'Really, the enthusiasm of your verbosity is overwhelming.' For a moment the officer was gobsmacked and then demanded, 'What does that mean? Is she swearing at me, because if she is, she's on report.' Our reply that it was straight English language made sure she said little to the inmate in future: having revealed her ignorance, she didn't want to draw too much attention to herself after that. It was quite an interesting incident, especially when viewed in the context of the new scheme which had just been introduced on the wing.

The Personal Officer Scheme meant that an officer was allocated an inmate for the purpose of aiding and helping out with any problems that inmate might have. Most of us felt this was a ludicrous idea. In theory it would relieve an overworked probation service of many problems and establish a deeper sense of trust and relationship between staff and inmates. In practice, the staff were perceived mainly as disciplinarians, and who wanted to place their trust in someone who had the power to deprive you of your privileges for engaging in some slight rule-breaking? How could anyone possibly relate to such officers as that in the above example? It is human nature for people to gossip, and the staff were no different; many inmates felt that their personal problems would be discussed between the staff, maybe trivialised and laughed over. They had no probation training and were not exactly expert psychologists. How could a twenty-three-year-old officer be mature enough to counsel someone of forty-three? Many of us refused to have a personal officer. Others felt it wasn't a bad idea and were prepared to give it a go, glad to have someone to relate to. I tried to maintain a balanced approach to the staff, treating them as they would me. I had no intention of discussing such personal matters as family problems with them and I viewed the scheme as intruding on my privacy. There has always been a tendency in prisons to view inmates as in some way belonging to the prison. In taking away all the freedoms of choice, decision and responsibility, and in control of you physically, it was as if the authorities now wanted to take over inmate's minds and know their innermost thoughts.

Amongst the inmates there was an unspoken agreement that if anyone did not wish to discuss either her crime or other personal details such as family, then that decision was respected. But there were inmates who wanted someone to discuss matters with, and many of us became listeners. They sometimes didn't want an inmate to give them advice, more to just listen and nod or shake one's head in the right places. Living together in close confines day after day, after a few years we began to be sick of the sight of each other and craved new and interesting company. The old saying 'Familiarity breeds contempt' often applied in H Wing. Many inmates were lifers or long-termers, which meant they stayed on the wing for up to four years before being transferred to other prisons. Sometimes the place was so quiet and the inmates so placid it felt like we would all sink into lethargy and sleep, like Rip Van Winkle, for twenty years. Knowing I had no chance of being transferred I had to find other ways in which to stimulate myself. I found it in the friends I made, inmates who, like me, felt the wing needed livening up now and again.

I usually preferred to have many acquaintances rather than a few firm friends. It was easier for me not to get too close to people who I knew would be moving on. In some way a part of me would go with them and I didn't have that much of me to spread around. Yet I did make friends, with women I have met up with since release and with others, still in prison, whom I visit. It's a fallacy that prisoners form close-knit groups according to their offence or length of sentence. Being a lifer, I did have friends who were lifers, but there were many I made friends with who were convicted of drug dealing, fraud or armed robbery and were serving sentences ranging from eighteen months to twelve or fourteen years.

Such as Khloud, who was a character altogether. A Member of the Palestine Liberation Organisation (PLO), she was serving twelve years for attempted murder of an ambassador. She had been born and lived in Beirut, and was heavily involved in the PLO, as was the rest of her family. Two of her brothers had been killed in action and one of her sisters had been killed leading a small combat unit in Israel. She was seventeen years old and had already killed a man, had been injured by a hand grenade and shot in the leg. It was very difficult for her to adjust to the cultural differences and she could not understand why the inmates did not stick together more. Having been in a situation where your very life is in someone else's hands and you, too, are responsible for the others with you, the lack of support amongst inmates was very frustrating and confusing for her.

I knew quite a bit of the history of the PLO and the Middle East and we would have conversations, sometimes heated, about how to resolve the situation over there. I used to wind her up as well. At first she was totally intractable over the word 'Israel', always referring to it as 'Palestine'. A friend had recently sent me a small rug for my cell. On unrolling it, I noticed that the label read, 'Made in Israel'. I chuckled to myself as a thought came into my head. Later that day, Khloud popped in for a chat and a coffee. I pointed out my new rug, inviting her to sit on it and feel how comfortable it was. She squatted down, crossing her legs, saying it was beautiful. I then pointed to the label. She jumped off the rug, calling me all the names under the sun. I could hardly stop laughing at her outrage. Eventually she saw the funny side and we ended up giggling over a cup of coffee and calling the rug names! I was, and still am, very fond of Khloud. When she was released she was deported by the Home Office to Algeria, where I hope to visit her some day soon.

Caroline, another friend, was serving a two-year sentence, for fraud, I think. A tiny firebrand, she could be stroppy and had a wild temper, which was checked sometimes by her great sense of humour. She had served a sentence some years earlier and was not enamoured of screws. During her first sentence her arm had been broken in a tussle with male prison officers whilst she was attempting to escape from Styal Prison.

We worked in the workshop, watched TV and ate together. There was also a great deal of conversation, which many times, understandably, turned to sex and men in general. I was pretty inexperienced compared to some of my companions, but I learned a lot from these discussions. Many of the lifers, who had been involved in 'domestic murders' – the murder of a husband or boyfriend – had little to say except what pigs their other halves had been. There were also women who had been happily involved in relationships and who spoke of them in glowing terms.

For most of the women simply talking about men provided a necessary release, whilst others formed attachments to fellow-inmates. Many of these were viewed as 'prison lesbians'. Women are normally more affectionate towards each other than men and because there was a deep lack of anything affectionate in prison, many women who would probably return to heterosexual relationships on release formed relationships with other women whilst in prison. There were also women who were real lesbians and shunned the 'prison' ones, seeking out a partner with whom they could continue the relationship after their release.

My friend Lorna was such. She was some years younger than me and I liked her because she was lively and interesting. She was serving a life sentence, but unlike most lifers who had been caught up in the routine, she had a naughty and mischievous streak to which I could relate, combined with a sly sense of humour. We got involved in all sorts of issues, some funny and some serious. Our relationship became one of deep friendship, based on trust, of which there is little in prison. I am usually affectionate by nature and think nothing of putting my arm around someone or giving them a hug. In prison this behaviour is frowned upon, viewed as 'abnormal', and is regarded as showing a possible tendency towards lesbianism. Which is quite ironic, since there exists a small percentage of 'lesbian' staff, many of whom never made any secret of the fact. 'Lesbian activities' amongst inmates are a punishable offence under the rule of 'good order and discipline'. Many women have found it extremely difficult to be physically affectionate towards their relatives and friends on release because of these attitudes. I think it's most unnatural to be viewed as 'deviant' if one spontaneously hugs or links arms with another woman. I would have liked to throw my arms around a man, but they are few and far between in a female prison and seldom interesting enough to excite my libido. I've yet to find one – but if Rutger Hauer is reading this book, please contact me!

Of course, we knew that there were hundreds of men just opposite, which led to shouted conversation at nights between the wings, sometimes accompanied by lewd and often obscene comments. Shouting out of the windows was a disciplinary offence in H Wing, so only a few women engaged in it. For most of us the idea of striking up a relationship based on loud conversation, which any inmate could listen to, was in some way a loss of dignity for both parties so we did not indulge. Apart from the fact that most of the males in the wing opposite were sex offenders, their language, at times, was obscene, and many of us found it repulsive. For the most part, though, the conversation was harmless and often quite funny, and some women found a penfriend to write to in the male prison.

The food in H Wing was abysmal, unpleasant looking, lacking in nutrition and tasteless. Meals were served on the 'Flat' where there were two rows of tables, with four inmates seated at each. We had no choice of table and were told where to sit by the officers. Even now, years later, I believe that in H Wing inmates still have to ask permission to move to another table. Meals, made by the male inmates in a large kitchen in their prison, were placed in large tins, which in turn were placed inside a large 'hot' trolley. This was wheeled to the outside wing gate; female inmates then brought it into our wing. The tins were placed inside a large hotplate until it was time for eating. Officers served the food from the hotplate and a large table placed next to it.

Breakfast was usually porridge, a few slices of bread, 'homemade', and either a boiled egg or a small, thin slice of bacon. Sometimes it was just toast with marmalade or jam. Tea was made on the wing by the women, as we had a large hot water urn on the flat. Most women hardly ate breakfast and lots of us made our own coffee and forgot food altogether. Dinner would be a slice of meat or fish, potatoes, usually boiled, sometimes mashed or, on Sundays, roasted. There was the inevitable cabbage (a vegetable I have never eaten since I was released) or mushy peas, both looking a little pale and worn out, the life boiled out of them. Dessert was usually a stodgy pudding with no sugar in it, or rice made with water and again no sugar. Tea would be a pie of some kind, chicken or steak and kidney; unfortunately, it all seemed to be cooked in some type of jelly or glaze. Beans or sausages and mash were served at other meals, also chips, which seemed to be the only thing the male inmates could cook properly. Supper consisted of a hot drink, nearly always tea (if you drank anything other than tea you had to provide and pay for it yourself) and a bun of some description which many of us didn't bother eating. One type on offer was hard and very yellow-looking, which we wittily nicknamed 'yellow-peril'. One night when it was 'yellow peril' for supper, I commented to a screw that you could probably kill someone if you threw the bun at them. She said

I was being ridiculous. I picked up the bun and threw it at the wall. It didn't even crumble, just fell to the ground, intact, with a thump. We were quite impressed. Of course, all institutional cooking is far from perfect, but it was unbelievable how good-quality food could be turned into such an unpalatable and unsavoury-looking mess. The daily budget for a prisoner's food is around 7p a day, which probably contributes to the lack of nutrition. Vegetables such as carrots or Brussels sprouts were rarely served, except on holidays. Not having a large appetite, the awfulness of prison food didn't really matter that much to me. I existed on bread, toast and biscuits and crisps bought with my wages.

After a few years, my body finally objected to this unappetising and less than nutritious fare. I woke one day with large red spots covering my legs and middle; they weren't irritable, just alarming. The doctor arranged for a dermatologist to see me. He was totally amazed: he said he'd only ever seen the like in a Third World country, and explained that it indicated a minor form of malnutrition. I was given, in pill form, large amounts of vitamins daily for about three months and the rash disappeared. A few years later it returned, and I was again given vitamins. At the time it was said that I acquired the rash because I didn't eat enough of the prison diet. Yet another inmate who ate most of the food put in front of her was eventually diagnosed as suffering from the same type of malnutrition. It's unfortunate that in prison the theory is to fill people up with stodgy foods, rather than attempting to provide nutrition, although with such a small food budget allowance most prison cooks would probably find it a challenge.

In 1984, Caroline, Lorna, Khloud and I decided to show our disapproval of the conditions in the hope that notice would be taken. Most inmates' disgruntlement is focused on the food they are given. Although, ironically, many of us had become almost indifferent to what was put in front of us, we used the resentment over poor food as a tool to highlight conditions in general. Supported by a women's group on the outside, we began a hunger strike. Knowing that not many would last any great length of time, we asked all the women to refuse meals, even for one day, whilst we gained some publicity. This was being arranged by the group called 'Women in Prison' which had been formed a few years earlier and whose members were mainly ex-inmates, some of whom had served part of their sentences on H Wing.

On the day in question, twenty-six women refused their meals. The press, already alerted, phoned the wing for details and so began a protest which called for conditions to be modernised and even for the closing of the wing on psychological grounds. Three days later there were only five of us still refusing meals: myself, Lorna, Caroline, Khloud and a lifer called Lisa. It wasn't a hunger strike in the sense that we were prepared to starve to death (although we didn't let the authorities know this), it was an attempt to better general conditions. Certainly the food was disgusting; what was even more disgusting was that it was ladled out of vast pans that looked as if they hadn't been properly cleaned in years. Other conditions we knew could be improved – hygiene, for instance. There were too many cockroaches and mice running about and we weren't allowed any disinfectant to help keep the place clean. All inmates agreed on the in-dignity of slopping out. On one level I can see why slopping out was an issue the Home Office would rather not take up. The prison service is always short of money and it would have been an expensive business to install toilets and wash-basins in every cell. Moreover – and this was probably the real problem – where would the inmates be housed while the plumbing was undertaken?

Solutions could have been found if there had been a real wish to improve things. Large sluices were available on every landing in H Wing for the inmates to slop out, large sinks where waste was emptied out and pots were washed out. The sluice on the ground floor often overflowed when the drains backed up and some mornings we would be greeted by large pools of water and waste flowing underneath the tables where we ate. It was totally disgusting and there were many rows when this happened because many of us refused to go down and mop it up. It wasn't until every inmate re-fused on one occasion and the officers themselves had to mop it up that anything was done about it. The sewer pipes were cleaned out, and have been ever since on a regular basis. That's all it took.

So it was over these issues that we carried on our hunger strike. It was quite exhilarating for us, as we felt, for once, completely in control. Hunger can make you light-headed anyway. The press regularly reported our weight loss and questions were asked in the Houses of Parliament about conditions on the wing. Obviously I felt hungry, but this lasted only for a few days. At that time I was already underweight, about 7st. 4lbs. and had earlier been prescribed a pint of milk a day by the doctor, which I shared with the other four striking inmates. One day I was called to the doctor, who threatened to withdraw my allowance. I told him it was OK by me, but suggested that it would look rather bad in the press if it was announced that five inmates were being deprived of one-fifth of a pint of milk a day. The milk allowance continued.

We ended our hunger strike three weeks later, the day after being informed that conditions were going to be improved. This news was related by a visitor who knew people in the Home Office and therefore could be trusted. We didn't achieve all we wanted: the wing still operates, slopping out is only now, as I write, being replaced by toilets and washbasins in the cells, but the food did improve noticeably. New tins and vats were bought, and the area, euphemistically termed 'the kitchen', which had previously held only two sinks, was modernised. A cooker and fridge were installed and two sandwich toasters bought. Although the main meals were still prepared in the male kitchen, we were allowed to buy food with our wages or private spends and make anything we liked in the kitchen during our association periods. It may seem a small victory to most people, but to us it was a major cause for celebration.

As I stated earlier, apart from the occasional fights and arguments which flared up, the majority of the time in prison, in H Wing especially, was quiet and boring, which resulted in lethargic lazing about and idle chatter. Now and again we would think up some scheme to liven the place and ourselves up. One day, Caroline had just returned from having a visit. Her visitors had given her flowers in a plant pot, inside which was an oasis, a spongy-type filling which absorbs water and keeps the flowers fresh. She had brought it to us, asking what we could do with it. After some thinking, we hit upon the idea of stuffing it in the keyholes of the cell doors. We broke it down into tiny pieces, then crept around the wing, avoiding staff and inmates, furtively sticking this stuff into a few of the keyholes. We weren't quite sure what the result would be, but it might prove amusing. It was. When the staff tried to lock the doors, their keys refused to turn, catching on this mass of oasis. We laughed to see them cursing and swearing, eyeing their locks in amazement. Eventually, the prison workmen were sent for and they cleared out the locks. It was an amusing episode for us and certainly gave everyone something to talk about for a few days. The staff never discovered who had done the deed, although they had their suspicions.

A couple of months later we decided to do it again, but on a grand scale. We went down to the kitchen area, where a couple of inmates were preparing to make a cake for their visitors. We asked them to lend us some flour, then took it away and mixed it with water. The result was a moist, flabby dough. Creeping round the prison we shoved it into every lock we could find, then sat back and waited. There was a couple of hours until bang-up at 8 p.m., so we reckoned it would be rock-hard by then. We were looking forward to bang-up time for a change. Five minutes before eight, the staff shouted at us to go to our cells. We stood outside, hanging over the railings, slyly observing through the suicide nets.

It was better than we had expected: some of the mixture was still gungy and attached itself to the keys as the staff placed them in the locks. Some doors wouldn't lock at all. The prison was in uproar as the inmates saw what was happening. From the third landing we had a good view of the chaos. Some inmates on the second landing were accused of doing it when the frustrated officer saw them laughing, which only made them laugh even more. The workmen were sent for, and some of us were still unlocked at around 8.30. We sat in the association cheerily chatting and laughing, while harassed workmen cursed and swore and staff eyed us suspiciously. We didn't care, it was one of the best laughs we'd had for a long time. One of the governor grades was called in and dire consequences were threatened when they found out who had perpetrated this wilful act. Safe in the knowledge that no one had seen us, we knew they couldn't do a thing and jeered at their aggression. For a short while, we – and they – realised, their control of us had been taken away. It infuriated and humiliated them: their security had been made insecure.

For days they cajoled the other inmates, threatening them with loss of association if they didn't tell them who had done it. But we three knew that if you want to do something outrageous and get away with it, don't tell another inmate. Still, the staff would make meaningful comments whenever we were around, hoping we would slip up and damn ourselves. We just smiled at them in satisfaction. We very rarely involved other inmates in our plots because of the danger of one 'grassing' to the staff. Grassing is a feature of prison life – inmates rarely stick together and support each other; 'honour among thieves' is obsolete. Most inmates and officers try to get along with each other because they have too many personal problems of their own without antagonising others and creating further hassle for themselves. It's a well-known fact that one of the duties of prison officers is to report whatever conversation they hear and be constantly aware of any trouble brewing. To this end they sometimes employ inmates to be their eyes and ears. These inmates are women who may not be very popular with the others for some reason or another. There are also some who become friendly with an individual officer and may, wittingly or unwittingly, reveal information. Others may be afraid of certain inmates and feel that by revealing information they are getting their revenge when that inmate gets punished. Prison is a devious place in which one listens to all the information given and reveals none of one's own unless necessary. It is a lonely existence for someone to choose to be a 'grass'. She is hated by inmates and may be subject to physical violence, but mostly she is ignored. Even though she may be helping the staff she is often despised by them. Aware of the grass, most inmates maintain a casual acquaintance with others and reserve talk of personal or illegal matters to their friends, so there is little feeling of group solidarity. Now and again, however, there would be a rare show of it, as the following incident shows.

The light switches in H Wing were outside the cells and in the control of the staff. Cell lights were usually switched off at 10 p.m. except for those of Cat A inmates. If you wanted to read after this time or have your light off before then you had to rely on an individual officer's decision. Most staff were quite agreeable to these requests, but one or two, mostly young officers, used it to establish control over the inmates and to satisfy their need for such power. One night just before lights out, Maureen, a lifer, asked the officer to switch off her light as she had a migraine. The officer, who was young and disliked by most inmates because of her attitude in general, demanded that Maureen say 'please'. It's bad enough that someone else can state when you can have your light on or off, it's even worse to have a silly young officer demanding, in a tone of derision, that you say 'please'. An argument developed, and as the wing echoes every raised voice, the rest of us could hear what was happening. Whether the inmates were outraged by the officer's derisory tones or whether they felt Maureen's sense of anger and frustration is a moot point. We all began to bang on our cell doors with whatever came to hand and ring the cell bells. The noise was overwhelming, especially when the male inmates shouted to find out what was happening and joined in. The deafening din brought a male security officer on to the wing and the female officer was severely told off for her stupid behaviour. The next morning half of us were placed on adjudication for causing a disturbance but the Governor decided not to punish us, and instead gave us a lecture on taking the law into our own hands. We informed him we would do the same if it happened again. It was a rare show of solidarity and for a while we all drew closer together, but it didn't last. Soon it dissolved into the more usual tenuous relationship.

Some years later another incident again resulted in some of the inmates coming together in a show of solidarity. It involved the same officer. I didn't take part in the vociferous complaint that preceded the incident. It was on a New Year's Eve, most of the staff were off duty and there was a skeleton staff of some three officers. They had just returned from their lunch break and the same young officer had obviously had too much to drink. Most of us were in the TV rooms watching a film; others were downstairs on the flat where it was decided a 'pyjama party' would be held. One of the older officers came into the TV room stating she was disgusted with this idea and the fact that the younger officer was parading around in some inmate's nightie and was drunk. I took no notice whatsoever, dismissing it as the stupid incident it was. A few days later though, it was revealed that a large number of inmates had complained about the officer, stating that they were worried that she was not responsible enough to look after them in a potentially life threatening situation such as a fire on the wing.

A member of the Board of Visitors interviewed inmates and took statements about the officer. I was approached because, even though I had not witnessed the incident, the fact that I had a reputation for speaking out and had been on the wing for some ten years would lend weight to the inmates' argument. I refused to write a statement, saying that the incident and the officer's behaviour was of no great import to me. I felt that I was quite old enough and able enough to look after myself in any situation and that I certainly wasn't dependent on any officer, young or old, to look after me. For ten years I had had to 'go it alone' and try and make sense and some kind of logic of my situation, and I had now got to the point where I was functioning almost independently of my surroundings.

In that year, 1984, the Home Office had a change of policy that would afford me even more independence. Permission was given for any inmate, including Cat As, to write and receive letters from anyone they wished. For ten years I had lived in a ghastly state of bored and resentful isolation, with a growing sense of injustice and rage, which sometimes caused me to suffer from depression. The Governor now made a decision to allow me to have visits at the same time as other inmates. This was not to improve my quality of life, but merely because there was a problem with visits in that when I had a visit no other inmate had one and there were often complaints that visiting times were too restricted. It helped a little: the small hubbub of conversation amongst the other tables gave a degree of privacy. Eventually the visiting room was refurbished. New, bright curtains were hung, a new carpet laid and easy chairs and coffee tables replaced the wooden ones. It was much easier and more relaxed, for both staff and inmates. For those who may think H Wing was going 'soft' on its inmates, I would like to remind them that an inmate's visitors are innocent of any crime and that many of them had travelled hundreds of miles and deserved a little comfort when they arrived. They, too, had their own problems. The following example shows how a prison sentence affects an inmate's relatives.

My sister came on a visit with my parents, bringing her four-year-daughter, Nancy. I, of course, was delighted to see them and we all had a good and enjoyable talk. Also having a visit then was another inmate, Sheila, a lifer, talking with her two small children and a relative. Nancy was eating sweets which I had bought for her from my wages. She wandered around the room, offering her sweets to us and the officers. Then she stepped across to where Sheila was sitting, and offered a sweet to the children. The little girl, about two years of age, took some. The little boy, aged about five, was not responding to his mother at all, drew back from Nancy and started crying. He then crouched in the corner and refused any attempts to console him. Sheila's visit was ended shortly afterwards, the child still sobbing on the way out, refusing to kiss his mother goodbye. Sheila told me he had been like this since she had been taken into custody and she was very distraught and worried. Inmates' families are deeply affected when their relatives are sent to prison. Some are greatly traumatised and end up on medication. Some never see the inmate throughout the sentence, due to lack of finances, or a sense of deep shame. It is hardly surprising that many relationships crumble and marriages break up during a prison sentence.

In 1986 I had to have a hysterectomy. Many people have questioned the high number of hysterectomy operations that women had whilst on H Wing and have viewed this as a result of the psychological pressures of life in such a small wing. To a point I would agree with this: women are far more emotional than men. They tend not to express their emotions outwardly and repress their fears and anxieties, which results in psychological problems, some of which affect the menstrual cycle. I was a late starter with periods, had never been regular and had never suffered any painful pre-menstrual symptoms. By 1986, however, the situation had radically changed. For some months I had been experiencing severe pain in my abdomen, so severe that I was injected with painkillers. These pains were not recognisably pre-menstrual, they occurred suddenly and violently and I would be laid up for hours at a time, unable to move until they faded. Sometimes it felt as if double-edged knives were twisting inside me, sometimes it was more like an ice-cold poker being forced through my abdomen. At the same time my periods began to go haywire: they would appear every two weeks, sometimes ten days apart, they were heavy and debilitating. I went to see the gynaecologist, who prescribed hormone pills. I took these for two months, then refused to take any more as they were having no beneficial effect; indeed, they seemed to be making the problem worse. After another visit to the gynaecologist, he suggested a D & C, yet three months after the 'scrape' the problem was as bad as ever. It is really terrible to be locked in your cell at night with little water to wash yourself when you have a heavy period.

I was becoming very tired and worn out and felt generally very unwell. The gynaecologist said he could do nothing other than a hysterectomy. I jumped at the chance: the immediate situation was such that I couldn't think in terms of never being able to bear children. Not knowing how long I would be in prison, my chances of bearing a child seemed very remote. I was nearly thirty-seven years old.

In early February I was told I was going to have the operation the following day at a hospital in Newcastle. The next morning I packed a few toiletries and went downstairs to await transport only to be horrified to learn that I would be handcuffed to the bed whilst I was in the hospital! I was disgusted: even though it was routine for Cat A inmates to be handcuffed to an officer if leaving a prison, I couldn't believe what I was hearing. A few weeks earlier, a male inmate had been escorted to hospital by two officers, who were then attacked by friends of the inmate who were helping him to escape. The Home Office then decreed that all Cat A inmates would, in future, be handcuffed at all times. The fact that I would have a very large wound in my abdomen and probably a drip attached to my arm wasn't to be taken into account. I refused to go, I shouted and cajoled, I cried at the very thought of it, all to no avail until the nursing sister who was accompanying us took me aside and said she would speak to the surgeon when we arrived at the hospital.

I arrived at the hospital, escorted by two female officers, one male officer, the nursing sister and four policemen in civvies, probably armed too. We were placed in a wing section: one room for me and the three officers in another, next door, for the police. When the surgeon arrived the sister explained the situation, whereupon he said no one was being handcuffed and if they insisted he would refuse to do the operation and they could take me back to the prison. After muttering amongst themselves they finally decided – no handcuffs. It was quite brave of them to make this decision without informing the Governor or the Home Officer, whose reaction no one could have gauged. Their decision also points to the fact that they did not consider me as dangerous as Cat As are supposed to be and that meant a lot to me, not only in terms of not being handcuffed, but also in terms of being treated with some humanity, based on trust.

I had the operation later that afternoon and spent the rest of the evening slowly coming round from the anaesthetic. In all I spent four days in hospital and at no time was I left alone in my room. There were always two female officers and one male on shift sessions of eight hours each, plus the four policemen, who popped their heads in once in a while and spent their days telling the poor nurses they had to give them a 'rub-down search' before they could enter the room. There was a TV in the room and our days were spent watching films or playing cards. The officers were very relaxed and treated the time as an enjoyable skive. They ensured I had nice food 'treats' and drink and brought me cigarettes, which they were not supposed to do.

The strangest thing happened on the day we arrived. A nurse placed a name tag on my wrist, which stated I was Jill Walker, or some such person. I was about to correct her when the nursing sister told me my name had been changed for 'security reasons'. All I can say is that it must have been something to see the nurses' faces after my op., when they tried to wake me from the anaesthetic. I did not respond to the name 'Jill' at all and they had difficulty wakening me, until the nursing sister called me by my own name and I began to stir! I recovered well and was returned to H Wing, where I was housed in the 'hospital'. This is a small segregated unit on the top floor of the wing, comprising three cells, an office opposite, used by the medical staff, and a small washroom with toilet and washbasin. For the next ten days or so I pottered about the hospital area, clutching my stomach in the mistaken belief that if I let go, my insides would fall out! I felt very fit and lively and ten years younger and, above all, clean at last. I have never regretted having the operation. Although I would have loved to have children, the strain and tension that I went through before the surgery was something I could not have borne for years on end. I have been asked if I feel any less feminine since having the operation: the answer is no, definitely not. I needed it and was glad to have it.

Most of the women in H Wing were worried about domestic problems they had left at home. 'She Wing', as it later became nicknamed, was regarded as nothing more than a nuisance by the largely male administrators of the prison who probably felt as uneasy with their relatively recent billet of women as the rectors of ancient universities felt about their first female students. They simply didn't know whether to treat us as the 'gentle sex' or as a curse of vicious, malign harpies who had invaded a traditional male stronghold. They viewed us as all-purpose 'difficult' women, although we were as diverse as any queue of women lining up with shopping at M & S or Sainsbury's: some would have bought white blouses, others red; some would buy Danish butter, others French.

The way in which women are sentenced, even nowadays, reflects this ambiguity of male opinion. Judges and society as a whole view women as either bad or mad. They don't see the shades of subtlety in between, and sentencing reflects this. The 'bad' women are punished more severely for their crimes than their male counterparts, particularly crimes of violence, it being seen as so unnatural that women should have perpetrated such acts. The 'mad' ones may get off more lightly but are often consigned to a psychiatric dustbin where their behaviour is, in an almost patronising way, explained by their hormones or their age. I suppose it must go back to old childhood conditioning: boys are allowed to be aggressive – it is almost expected – whereas girls are still supposed to be dainty, biddable and other-cheek-offering. Assertiveness is viewed as a male-only area, a theory reflected in the attitudes of the judge who says that sometimes when a woman says 'no' to sexual intercourse, she may mean 'yes'. Or the judge who said it was fine to slap a woman around a little, but bone-breaking force was out of order, and proceeded to give the male defendant a conditional discharge after assaulting a woman; and the judge who recently thought that £500 towards a good holiday was sufficient compensation for a fifteen-year-old girl who had been raped. The prison system reinforces these attitudes. Ironically, women found guilty of an offence that is deemed sufficiently serious to deprive her of her liberty, women considered to be serious risks to society, can still be addressed in hollowly courteous or dismissive terms. Any outburst of temper or frustration was frowned upon as 'unladylike', while most of the educational classes were geared towards such pursuits as needlework, cookery, child-care and home economics. These attitudes are beginning to change, albeit slowly, and courses such as computing, science and technology, accountancy and business studies are no longer viewed as a strictly male province. More importantly, the Home Office is beginning to recognise the value of education. I feel that not enough funding is put into this department by the Home Office and it is quite noticeable that any internal cutbacks always effect education first. Why wasn't (and isn't today) more money spent on education? I suppose I can answer my own question fairly easily.

There is a quotation that 'a little learning is a dangerous thing'. The staff, from the Governor down to the most lowly officer, were well aware that education of prisoners can result in loss of control over them. (Thank God, this attitude seems to be changing nowadays). An inarticulate person cannot ask a searching question or produce a logical argument. For the authorities it was preferable for inmates to resort to violence or churlish silence, which made them more controllable. It is much easier and quicker to lock someone in a cell than enter into a logical discussion which might result in such questions being asked as: Why is so much money wasted in the prison service? Why did they install state-of-the-art equipment in the workshop where so many of us toiled when few of us, if any, had the slightest intention of working as machinists upon release? Why did perfectly good office furniture have to be expensively changed and, I was informed, dumped when new officers came to work in H Wing? We could easily have put to use some of the items or the money they could have fetched second-hand. Members of staff, some of whom have little real authority, do not want to be asked difficult questions because their inability to answer them, and their own sense of powerlessness to influence events, becomes too humiliating. After two or three years in H Wing I began to study and to prove to other people – but more importantly to myself – that I was not some lost pea-brain. In the meantime I busied myself with other issues, one of which was Christmas.

Christmas was not a time we looked forward to. There was no work for about ten days, as staff and workshop instructors were anxious to be with friends and families. Most inmates thoughts inevitably turned towards their own families and friends. It seemed as if the whole Christian world was celebrating, except for prison inmates who were stone-cold sober and bored stiff, with not even the workshop in which to pass the tedious hours.

There was always a carol service, although what pleasure anyone imagined it would give to a belligerent choir of cons to lift up their voices and celebrate the birth of Baby Jesus to a small group of staff and other inmates I cannot think! The service was usually held on the ground floor of the wing, with an audience of inmates, staff and perhaps some member of the Board of Visitors. Hot drinks and sandwiches were served afterwards and we 'mingled' in small groups, talking inanities. Years later, we were allowed to have the service in the main chapel, outside the wing, which earlier was used only by the men. This was quite a step: and many of us put on our best togs and slapped on make-up for the event. We tottered on our high heels over to the chapel, accompanied by the wolf-whistles and cat-calls from the male inmates whose wing we had to pass. I used to attend or not, as the feeling took me. The alternative was to be locked in my cell for the evening, and sometimes I took this option when it became apparent that the whole celebratory aspect was beginning to verge on the hysterical. Few of us looked forward to Christmas dinner: always some identifiable slice of turkey, usually from a roll, sprouts and plum pudding. To give credit, the kitchen guys did their best and sometimes turned out a very passable dinner, yet the brevity and paucity of our celebration often made us feel more miserable.

One Christmas was even more depressing than usual. All morning we'd scrubbed and polished, the wing was gleaming, we were looking forward to the afternoon off, it was Christmas Eve. If you looked down from the landings through the suicide netting, you could see garish decorations all along the walls of the flat. The tree, with fairy lights twinkling, echoed everyone's mood, we were even whistling and laughing as we went down for dinner. An hour later the peace and quiet was broken by the call of 'Fire!' We ran out of the landings and saw thick, black smoke curling from a doorway from a cell on the top landing. An inmate, Susan, had asked to be locked in for a while, claiming she didn't feel well, had set fire to her mattress and then blocked the door with her bed. Susan had always been regarded as a threat. Sentenced to seven years for arson, she had recently arrived in H Wing after several years in Rampton top security mental hospital. No one knew why she had been sent to our wing. We had already been warned that we were not to give her matches, with a threat that we would be severely punished if it was discovered that we had.

Panic was beginning to set in. Although the walls of H Wing are thick stone and there was no real danger of anyone else getting hurt, the fact that we were enclosed in such a small wing, coupled with the thought that an inmate might actually be burning to death, did little to calm the situation. Some women became hysterical and had to be slapped into submission; some sobbed, some just stood staring. As it was the dinner period, there were only three officers on duty and a nursing sister. They tried to get Susan's door open while I and two or three others ran for fire buckets and extinguishers, which are situated at the end of each landing. We ran up the stairs, hauling buckets, with water slopping over the sides down on to the flat below and the Christmas tree. The water hit the electric lights and caused more panic as the lights began to flicker. Orders were shouted to pull plugs and most of the inmates told to go down on the flat, accompanied by one of the officers. The rest of us tried to push open the door.

Fortunately, the door had a small hatch in it. We pulled it down, aimed the extinguisher hose at the fire on the bed, and quenched the flames, soaking ourselves in the process. Finally the door gave in under the force of people pushing and the officers went in and grabbed Susan, dragging her out on to the landing. We were relieved to see she wasn't hurt, just dirty from the smoke. With the panic now over, relief turned to anger. She had ruined our cleaning, scared us out of our wits, and we were furious. Two of us, still holding the extinguishers, soaked her with water, calling her all the silly bastards under the sun. The officers took her off to the punishment cell and the rest of us were escorted out of the wing and into the workshop. The fire service had to be called, as with any fire in a prison. For the next couple of hours we sat in the workroom, discussing the incident and wondering who had given her the matches. Recriminations passed back and forth and the atmosphere was despondent, especially when we returned to the wing. It was a mess. The smell of smoke was everywhere, ashes from the burnt mattress had mingled with the water from the buckets and extinguishers. There was nothing else to do except get stuck in and clean the place all over again.

We were supposed to be having a disco later that evening, although nobody felt much like dancing. However, the scrubbing and polishing got rid of our apathy and we began to look forward to a bit of a disco after all – especially when we found out the matches had been given to Susan by an officer! The day before we had been paid our weekly wages, Susan had written down what she wanted and had included matches. The officer had forgotten she wasn't supposed to have any and had handed them over to her.

Disco time came and everyone started to feel the music. It was hard to believe that the fire had happened at all; the

women danced with a frenzy, as if trying to purge themselves of the whole incident. Soft drinks, cakes and biscuits
were consumed with a passion. A couple of officers even
took some of the goodies up to Susan in the strip cell. She
had been forgiven by all of us: we knew she wasn't the 'full
shilling'. The officers wished her goodnight and a Merry
Christmas for the following day, asking if there was anything
she needed. She replied no, and they locked the door. A few
moments later a voice rang out, 'Oh Miss, do you think I
could have a light for my fag?'

In the first few years, Christmas festivities were organised
by the staff. Disco dances and bingo were the usual projects.
One year, depressed at the thought of yet another session of
bingo, I suggested to a few women that we might try and put
on a concert. The idea took off and every year, as September
drew to a close, we would be involved in a hive of activity,
organising dancers, mime artists, singers, music and cos-
tumes and arranging rehearsals. Some of the concerts were
really good: the talent that sometimes exists in prison is truly
remarkable. Some were not so good, but I enjoyed the organisation and viewed it as a challenge. We thought long and
hard each year to try and be original and outdo former acts.

At first we were allowed to have a small quantity of cigarettes, sweets and fruit sent in by our relatives or friends at
Christmas, but this was stopped after a couple of years. I
think mainly due to worries about drugs being sent in
amongst the foodstuff, although it was all checked by staff
before being issued. Not content with this, a few of us
thought about starting up a collection every year. We asked
each inmate to donate a small amount of wages, maybe 20p a
week. As wages had risen it wasn't considered too expensive. This was put into a kitty from September onwards. In
mid-December we would ask permission for a member of
staff to go and purchase sweets and cigarettes with the
money collected. I thought it was quite a good idea as there
were inmates who didn't have much of a wage and some of
us were by then on piece-rate wages. There were also those
who had no private money and could not buy themselves
any food for Christmas; if you had private money you would
be allowed to use a certain amount to purchase extra treats at
this time.

In the meantime, we made Christmas stockings out of old material and the sweets and cigarettes were divided up, each inmate receiving at least one little 'present'. There was also a quiet show of Christmas spirit, when one inmate would pay double because another didn't have enough of a wage to afford even the 20p a week.

Along with Christmas comes religion. I am not a bit religious and attended Mass only a few times, but many inmates seemed to gain some inner peace and strength from their faith. Others did not attend any service as the overall impression of religion in prison is that it is a carrot made for parole, and there is a heavy emphasis on 'repentance of sins'. The Salvation Army used to come round, as did other religious groups. In the main they were viewed as purely entertainment and little else. It was almost a relief when Christmas was over. Everyone was prone to feelings of loss, disappointment and loneliness, as people do outside, probably more so at Christmas than any other time of the year.

If the organising of concerts and other events was a challenge to me, it also proved a bitter irony. My ability to stir my fellow-inmates was seen as evidence of my subversive power, especially as I was convicted of a 'politically motivated' crime. Just as I had been viewed as something of a control-freak during the hunger strike, I was now seen as a motivator and manipulator. If I could organise women to participate in a concert, I could organise a riot. This attitude infuriated me, I was not a goody-two-shoes by any means, but there was no way I would get involved in anything like a riot. I could be a bolshie little bastard and was quite prepared to stand up for myself and for others who, for many reasons, couldn't do the same, and I was annoyed and irritated that the authorities couldn't see that my 'organising' was more a means of survival than a threat to others.

This was just one of the many issues which caused friction and irritation. In movies about prison it is usually on the exercise yard that scams are made, plots are hatched and schemes are planned. H Wing's exercise space was too small for this: any suspicious-looking grouping would immediately draw the staff's attention. For the allotted hour we would tramp round the bleak tarmac, sometimes chatting, sometimes silent. Many women would not go out in winter, apart from the cold, the yard was a depressing place with its high fencing, barbed wire and security cameras. Summer was a different matter and most of us would take great enjoyment in the hour's sunshine. Sometimes at weekends we would be allowed extra 'exercise' periods in the afternoons. Many of us would slap skin lotions on our arms and faces, in the hope of acquiring a little colour. At the same time as trying to colour our bodies, we coloured our minds with talk of release. As people outside hope that they will get a better job, or be able to afford a holiday, so we hoped for release. Of course, there were those with determinate sentences, who knew exactly when they would be released, if they didn't get parole. If an inmate is serving a sentence of perhaps, six years, she would be reviewed for parole after two years. If no parole was granted, she would at least know that, with good behaviour, she would certainly be released after four years.

For lifers, though, thoughts of parole were highly important. There was no time off for good behaviour for a lifer. There were various theories on why an inmate was granted parole: a belief that good behaviour counted, and that if you had a job to go to and living accommodation, your chances of parole would be good. There was also a common belief that parole was a lottery, that Home Office ministers wrote the names of those inmates due for parole on slips of paper, placed them in a bin, gave it a shake and the first four or five names pulled out were those who got it. This may seem like a bleak joke, but such was the cynicism that many, including myself, believed it. We could never figure out why a certain inmate got parole and another didn't. If you were refused parole, the reason was never stated, giving rise to speculation that the Home Office people themselves were never sure of the reason for and against parole for an individual inmate. I always hoped that one day I would be released. Who doesn't? Just how it would come about or when was more shadowy. I just clung to a belief that, one day, I too would walk through those gates.

We sat and gossiped and the politics that exist in any office, let alone a closed society, were aired. An inmate was being bullied by another – should we do something about it? If so, was it right to sort it out ourselves or should the staff be informed? Should we complain about the stifling heat in the workroom and ask for air conditioning to be put in or should we all refuse to work in there? More often than not, especially in the summer, we were just content to lie and sit around and soak up the sun; no one wanted to spoil the coveted hour by muttering over troubling things. Civilisation finally came to the exercise yard and wooden benches were installed. Instead of sitting on our jackets we could now relax in relative comfort.

If it was raining or snowing, we were never allowed out and had to go to the blue room. Here, when the weather was inclement, we played badminton and rounders and, besides being an indoor exercise area, it was also a gym. Once or twice a week we were allowed a two-hour period of gym. Few inmates attended but I went, mainly to relieve the boredom of the workshop. We did aerobics and general fitness exercises. Later, proper gym equipment arrived and I enjoyed throwing myself about on the trampoline and diving on to large floor mats. I entered some of the gymnastic and trampoline courses and still have the badges and certificates, proof of my once great skills. I admit to thoroughly enjoying it, to such an extent that a few of us brought keep-fit tapes and records such as those of Jane Fonda and spent our evening hours in mad sessions of aerobics. We adapted our aerobic and gymnastics to music and incorporated them into our concerts; these were the times when, I think, we were most content. We suffered our sweating bodies and panting lungs, but gained great satisfaction and, more importantly, it was a great way of releasing tension.

One way to cut down on stress was to immerse oneself in films on TV. We had two black-and-white TVs in H Wing and were allowed to watch TV in the weekday evenings from 5 to 8 p.m. As there was no work at weekends we were allowed to watch from 12 noon until 8 p.m. I didn't watch much during the early years; weekend TV was mostly sport, so I spent my time either chatting or reading. Later on, colour TVs replaced the black-and-whites and a video machine was purchased. One inmate was responsible for using the video, taping programmes requested by the inmates. Mostly, films were taped, although documentaries and OU programmes

were occasionally requested. On programmes like *Prisoner,
Cell Block H* it is irritating to see prison life portrayed in such
black-and-white terms. They only show victims and oppres-
sors, whether officers or inmates. Sometimes there is the
caring, kindly Googie-Withers-type headmistressy governor,
whose heart is fashioned from pure gold, even though her
task is onerous and difficult. *Within These Walls* was a TV programme which was popular when I was first banged up and
reflected my reality, just as *Dixon of Dock Green* reflected the
popular image of the straightforward bobby who dealt with
the criminal classes but was happy to report to relieved view-
ers at the end of each episode that the villain had 'gone
straight'. This is what the public were led to believe; they
could not conceive any other view without being informed of
the facts and there is little enough real information on these
subjects.

Prisoners in programmes such as *Cell Block H* are stereo-
types, as were those portrayed in *Porridge*. Funny though
that programme was at times, it often made prison seem like
a cross between St Trinian's and everyday office politics.
Prison is not entirely populated by charming old lags,
scrapes and dim-witted officers . . . they all exist, but so do
the nastier aspects.

Violence will always exist in a system in which there are
continually changing rules. A high ratio of prison officers to
inmates, a strong emphasis on security, cramped accommodation and lack of physical outlet are all factors which
contribute to the barely concealed tensions of prison life.
They provide fodder to insecure inmates already frustrated
by their own seemingly insoluble problems. Women have
physically attacked others because they have been refused
parole, or even just because they feel particularly tense and
have a need to release pent-up emotions. Staff have been
attacked due to the glowering resentment often felt as a result of the enforcing of some petty rule. Women needing
psychiatric help pose their own, different problems. In the
main, they are sad, depressed, harmless souls, but occasionally there is one who is dangerously violent and to be
avoided, if possible – not easily done when you're all locked
in a small workshop. Such disturbed women created a great

deal of tension in H Wing, as most of us were unsure whether they were likely to be violent or not and their disturbed outpourings and actions saddened and frustrated us in turn.

One poor woman, Jackie, dismantled her cell. I say dismantled and mean just that: she ripped the sheets and blankets into small pieces, smashed and broke the locker and wardrobe and tore most of her clothing to bits, including the ones she was wearing. She had completely flipped out, for what reason no one knew, and she was placed in a strip cell on the top landing. In H Wing this is just a cell which is stripped of furniture and bed, with only a mattress on the floor and two 'strip' blankets left in. The blankets are thick and nearly indestructible. The inmate's clothes are removed and she is given a 'strip dress' to wear. This is a short, coarse piece of material in the shape of a smock-type dress, without buttons or ties, little more civilised than a straitjacket.

Jackie was drugged heavily to calm her down; unfortunately the medication made her sleep all day and left her awake most of the night. The rest of us, having been awake all day, were looking forward to our night's kip, but Jackie ensured we got very little of this. Every night, Jackie would scream and shout at the officers: 'Open the door, you bastards, or I'll kill you!', and other less polite remarks. If this wasn't bad enough, she then acquired a habit of counting down the time they had to open the door. 'I'm going to count to ten and if you don't open this door . . . '. Then she would begin, 'Ten, nine, eight . . . '. The rest of us would be lying in our cells, counting along with her, 'Seven, six, five . . . ', and so on. Upon reaching 'one', she would scream manically and pound on the door violently.

We had to put up with this, every night, for about ten weeks. We became snappy and irritable due to loss of sleep and angrily demanded of the nursing staff what was being done about her. They were waiting for a bed for her in one of the local mental hospitals. I remarked that they would probably need another forty by the time she went! Jackie was a big woman and the staff told me that because of her size and mental state, the medication they were giving her, which would have floored any of the rest of us, was having little effect. She smeared her faeces over the floor and wall, refusing to use the pot, and talked frequently to people and animals she 'saw' in her cell. We had quite a laugh over an incident concerning Jackie's 'companions'.

One day, Jackie told the staff she had a dog in her cell and described its colour and size and even its name. This imaginary dog seemed to have some calming influence on her. So that evening, when one of the night officers arrived, the day staff told her this. The night officer went up to say good evening to Jackie and, hoping that if she mentioned the dog, Jackie might remain calm for the night said to her, 'Oh, Jackie, that's a lovely dog. What's its name?' Jackie glared at her for a few seconds and retorted, 'You're off your fucking head, you. There's no bleeding dog in here!' It gave us all a laugh for days and we wound up the officer mercilessly. Jackie was eventually transferred to hospital. There was always a small percentage of disturbed women in H Wing, although in other prisons mentally disturbed inmates are usually segregated on their own hospital wings. I don't know whether this is a good idea or not, but these inmates certainly made living in such a small space very uncomfortable and tense.

I have never attacked anyone physically, although I often felt like it. I discovered the violence of words. A meaningful look could also convey anger or disgust. I often punched the wall, or pounded the much-maligned furniture in my cell to release my emotions, leaving a legacy of battered lockers and unhinged wardrobe doors, which I wouldn't be surprised to discover are still in use in H Wing! There is also the violence of death.

Maria was in her late thirties, serving a seven-year sentence for manslaughter. She was Hungarian and came to live in England after marriage to an Englishman. He had, we heard from an officer, abused her physically and mentally over a period of years. They had a small son, aged about five. After some years, the woman could stand it no more: she gave her son sleeping tablets and took the rest herself. Some hours later, she woke in hospital. Her son never woke at all. She was a quiet, depressed woman, slight in stature. She crept round the wing, making little impression on the community in general. In the early hours of one Saturday morning, her son's birthday, she hanged herself. It was the first death on H Wing and everyone, staff and inmates, were shocked and saddened. For a couple of days, the wing was quiet. I think we all felt some form of collective guilt that we hadn't taken much notice of her, hadn't really extended the hand of friendship and companionship, which she may have needed. Although life returned more or less to normal, a few of us often thought about her. I can still see her face, sad and lined, her grey hair and dark clothes perhaps reflecting her depression.

There were times, though, when the violence was mixed with humour. One morning a fight began over the breakfast tables. A young inmate, Mary, had a crush on one of the young officers. At this time, there were 'sleeping-in' night duty officers. Two small cells on the top floor had been converted into a bedroom and bathroom for the screw who slept overnight. She was there to assist the official night duty officers in case of emergency. The inmate who was cleaning on the top landing was responsible for keeping these rooms clean and changing the sheets. Mary was that inmate; the night before she had made an 'apple-pie' bed for the young officer as a joke.

The following morning, the officer was standing near the breakfast area. Mary called her, asking, 'Did you get cramps in your legs last night?' The officer laughed. Another inmate, Jane, didn't like either Mary or the officer and decided to make it known. She shouted out, 'Pity it wasn't her fucking neck!' Mary took umbrage and threw a breakfast plate at Jane. In seconds a major fight erupted. Tables were pushed out of the way, cups and plates flew through the air as friends of both women joined in. The officers ran to stop the affray, and breakfast was definitely over! Some inmates shouted their encouragement or disgust, others cowered out of the way, afraid. Most of us carried on eating, enjoying the respite from boredom.

Anne Maguire, who at that time was seated at one of the top tables and had not seen such violence since coming to H Wing, was panic-stricken and became a little hysterical: more, I think, at the speed of how the fight erupted than about any threat to herself. Some of the inmates pulled her away from the fight into a corner. The breakfast area was in the shape of an L, with the majority of tables situated at the longer end, the gate to the wing being at the shorter end. Anyone entering might be unaware of what was happening at the other end. The 'aggro bell' was rung, to summon assistance from some very beefy male officers. Moments later four or five of them piled through the gate. They couldn't see the fight round the corner; all they saw was four or five women trying to calm Anne down, so they made a beeline for this group. Anne saw them coming, went totally hysterical and began screaming. With others, I called to the men they were going the wrong way, although we could hardly speak we were laughing so much. Anne's face, upon seeing those burly men rushing at her, is a picture that still gives me a chuckle. She herself laughs at the recollection. The men restored order, with the fighting group escorted to their cells, to be banged-up and adjudicated on the following day. The rest of us cleaned up the crumbled pieces of toast and spilt tea, comparing notes on what we had seen of the fight. To those not familiar with the violence of prison, Anne's predicament and fear may seem tragic. Yet no one had been seriously hurt, except for a certain loss of pride, and we saw the whole episode as an interesting and humorous diversion in another boring breakfast. Much of the violence in prison is neither serious nor threatening, although I have heard of incidents which, even in prison terms, are shocking. One involved a lover's tiff between two lesbian women, where a woman's face was badly cut; in another, drugs were involved and three women violently assaulted a fourth, who had concealed drugs inside her vagina.

Drugs were never a big issue for me. I have smoked and enjoyed joints in my time, but could always take them or leave them. There weren't that many available in H Wing, although you could often find a joint if you knew the right people. Hard drugs such as pills or heroin were virtually unknown. In the late 1970s and early 1980s many women had come to H Wing serving sentences for drug dealing or smuggling. A sentence of seven years was seen as way over the top then, unlike the twelve, fifteen and more, years regularly handed down by the courts today. Most of the women I knew then were young, involved in drug-dealing cartels and have travelled widely throughout the Middle East, South America and Europe. They told us outrageous tales of their smuggling, their antics in avoiding customs officers and drug squads. There were tales of people beaten up for not delivering the goods, even murdered, with hands and heads chopped off to avoid identification. These women were vivacious and lively, unrepentant of their crimes, and thoroughly enjoyed their lifestyle. For them the prison sentence was somewhat of a respite from their hectic 'civvy' careers. They were a complete contrast to women I met later in Holloway.

9

Cookham Wood, Holloway, Durham, 1987–90

The year 1987 was one of change for H Wing and for me. By now the blue room had been refurbished as a proper gym, with wall bars, flooring and equipment. It was great for us and we spent hours working our way to fitness doing gymnastics or aerobics and trampolining. The old entrance gate to the prison was closed up and a new gatehouse was built at the side of the prison almost adjoining our wing. It created more suitable room for visitors, inmates and staff alike. Most of the administration offices were also placed there: it was quite a forward move for Durham. The only blight on the proceedings was the discovery of some skeletons when the foundations were being dug, probably some poor sods who had been hanged in the 'good old days'! We had also been informed of future proposals to install toilets and washbasins in all the cells, although this wouldn't be effective immediately.

Around 12 noon on that day I was in a friend's cell, chatting through the dinner hour association, when I was called to the Wing Governor's office. A well-suited bod from the Home Office was there, who had come to the prison for the official opening of the gatehouse. He informed me I was no longer classified as Category A. I think he expected me to sink to my knees, kiss the hem of his trousers and say three Hail Marys. My first reaction was: 'So what? It doesn't set me free. There was also the slight niggle regarding the whole process of Category A and how the Home Office decides that you are no longer a 'danger'. At 11.55 a.m. I'm regarded as a threat to national security and at 12.06 p.m. I'm an ordinary con, with the chance to move to a less secure and more open prison. What has happened to effect this change? I hadn't changed that radically. I'd got some education, grown a little older and more or less kept to the rules. I'd almost given up hope of being decategorised some two years earlier, when I had a conversation with a senior officer after one of the yearly reviews on my Category A status. Before these reviews, the staff were required to write reports on me, which would be sent to the Home Office for perusal before any decision was made. This officer had told me that the Home Office had said they wouldn't decategorise me because I'd been on H Wing so long that the staff were writing reports in my favour. All staff are supposed to write neutral reports on individual inmates and the Home Office felt that the staff on H Wing were being less than neutral either because I'd manipulated them or because they felt sorry for me. In actual fact it was neither. They had merely said that they felt it was now the time for me to be decategorised and transferred elsewhere as they had nothing else to offer me on H Wing. I had outlived the facilities they could offer some time ago and there was no point in my remaining there longer. It was a Catch 22 situation: in order to go to another prison I had to be decategorised as there were no other top-security wings for women in the country, yet I wasn't to be decategorised because the staff wrote favourably for my transfer to another prison. Who was supposed to write the reports if not the staff, and if no reports were written, how was I to get decategorised? So, in the light of that information, the decision to decategorise me was of great interest. I've never discovered how it was arrived at. However, I was now your ordinary con. I still wasn't free and would not be for several more years, but my life was beginning to change. I could now think about a transfer.

There were only two options in 1987: either Styal in Cheshire or Cookham Wood in Kent. Styal, I discovered, was out of the question, Carole Richardson had been transferred there some years earlier and the authorities weren't keen to have two 'high-profile inmates' in the same prison. I wouldn't have gone there if I had had the option, even though it was only a short distance from where my parents lived. Styal is run on a sort of housewifey basis. It consists of a series of 'houses', with maybe 20 to 25 inmates in each.

There are no cells in most of the houses, although there is a punishment house and a 'lock-up' house, which is used for those who can't function in the ordinary houses. Two or three, maybe more, inmates share a room. There are few single rooms and I was used to my privacy by now. The policy is to run the prison on the lines of a 'normal' day, with inmates leaving the house for work, returning for meals, and so on. The grounds are beautiful and there are far more facilities than in H Wing. However, there are also some very petty rules. You can't walk on the grass, you can't smoke in the bedrooms, you can't go upstairs until a certain time and the only place to sit is in the lounge. To try and equate this with 'normal' everyday living in the outside world seemed ludicrous, and I felt that life there would be too stifling.

Cookham was a relatively new prison. Around ten years old then, it was supposed to be liberal and have good facilities for a better quality of life. I was told I would be able to work outside in the gardens and attend the local swimming pool. The education facilities were said to be much of an improvement on H Wing's. However, I wasn't to move from H Wing until some seventeen months later. I spent my last months there in increasing impatience. Being decategorised resulted in some small improvements in my living. I was now allowed to carry the food in from the outside gate, clean all week on the flat if I desired; no more escort of officers, no more accompanying black book. I was no longer subject to frequent cell changes. The feeling of being observed was drastically reduced. Most important of all, I could now have my light off all night.

That first night I pulled my curtains tightly together, and great was my contentment when the light went off at 10 p.m. and stayed off. I was allowed to move to a different cell. This was on the top landing of the wing and there was a view of the town, rooftops and trees. This made bang-up time a lot more pleasant. Around this time I had my ears pierced. I would like to say that this was in prophetic anticipation of a move to the relative freedom of larger prison. Not so. A friend had sent me a pair of gold earrings; they were pretty and I thought it was a shame not to wear them. I asked one of my friends inside if she would pierce my ears: she took her darning needle, 'sterilised' it in a cup of boiling water from the urn and a minute later I had pierced ears. It didn't hurt at all, even though it does sound a little barbaric. One ear became slightly infected so I went to the nurse, who gave me some ointment. I could have got into trouble: technically I had committed the offence of self-mutilation, but the nurse was a reasonable woman, she gave me some stuff and turned a blind eye. Small matters to others, but ones which made me feel like I was moving towards being a real person again.

Another great improvement, not just for me but for all on H Wing, was the arrival of a new governor, Martin Mogg, or 'Uncle Martin', as I dubbed him. We never took too much notice of new governors arriving, there had been some five or six before him in my years there. The difference was that this man not only thought liberally, but also put his thoughts into actions. As I said earlier, the workshop was, at best, boring and offered nothing in terms of interest and quality of life. The Governor agreed with us on this point and forwarded the idea of the inmates forming a small business. The machines were removed, staff and inmates sat together to formulate ideas – an improvement in itself. The result was the partitioning off of the workshop into small sections: two taken up for educational purposes, one for computers and desktop publishing, others for pottery and art and the making of soft-toy products, any profit from which would be put back into the business. It was a major step for H Wing. There was some opposition from both staff and inmates in the beginning. I couldn't understand this, especially from the inmates, but saw that they perceived it as a threat, as did the staff, to the routine they had succumbed to. They felt they couldn't cope with this new and exciting challenge. Courses were set up so the inmates would understand the ins and outs of running their own businesses. I didn't attend any of these, as I thought I might be transferred before finishing the course. In fact, I could probably have finished two courses, as an issue was arising in the Home Office over my transfer. I had no idea of this but it was to keep me longer than intended on H Wing.

As my fourteenth Christmas on H Wing approached, I was seized with a great anxiety to be gone. I had exhausted the

facilities or outlets the wing could offer. I had sat and passed
three RSA exams in English language, computer literacy and
information technology, and maths. I had passed four O
levels, in Spanish, art, English and history, and one A level,
in English literature. I did a correspondence course in
English and journalism and won a small Koestler award for a
short story I wrote about my life with horses. The Koestler
award was set up by Arthur Koestler, especially to encourage
creative arts among prisoners. I was also in the final eighteen
months of an Open University degree course, specialising in
European history. Of course I didn't get to go to any of the
summer schools, which the OU usually expects of its
students, but I don't feel that I really missed out. I passed in
1989 and got my degree. I do have a sense of pride in achiev-
ing all I did, although at first I involved myself in education
merely to escape the monotony of life on the wing. However,
after the first year or so, I really enjoyed it, especially the
great sense of achievement that results from exams being
taken and passed. I was greatly excited on hearing that I had
passed my first exam: it was the first time I'd passed anything really important to me.

At this time I was involved in and fascinated by computers. Before the changes of the new workshop, two
computers had arrived on the wing and at first there was
only myself and another inmate who took any great interest
in them. In fact I'm probably the only person in the world
stupid enough to have read all the accompanying manuals
from cover to cover! This was ignorance of the computer
rather than any desire to learn all the technical aspects, but I
can now use computers in a more comprehensive fashion
due to this intensive perusal. The only other inmate who had
definite computer skills was Eva, an East German woman
who had been charged with spying. She was released when
the Berlin Wall came down and détente was restored. People
– especially some of the education staff – thought it slightly
disturbing that the two of us, regarded as 'politicals', should
be immersing ourselves in these technical codes. Eva had a
gruff manner that was frequently misunderstood. She taught
me a smattering of German and I knew – though most of my
companions didn't – that what sounds like barking arrogance

in a literally grammatical translation of the German is perfectly courteous and polite. But Eva, I'm afraid, was viewed as bossy and rude in her attempts to be civil in English.

I had also got involved in work for the blind. In the early 1980s, a probation officer had brought a braille machine and instruction book to the wing and asked who would like to have a go. Braille being entirely new to me, I took it on. It was completely absorbing. I had a machine, something like a typewriter, but with only six keys. By punching a combination of the six keys you formed the braille language. At first I transcribed children's books for a blind school in Newcastle which, sadly, closed after a few years. I was then approached by the OU to transcribe material for their blind students. Much of the material was science or technology and there was a problem at first with how to describe diagrams. As you may imagine, the task of translating a visual diagram into something that can only be understood by the touch of a finger on the raised dots of braille is quite a challenge. I got in touch with the Royal National Institute for the Blind and they sent me special tools for making diagrams. Although this helped greatly, there were still some that had to be 'written', as it were. I found that I needed to think 'blind' to anticipate the difficulties and adapt not only the words but the visuals themselves, and the way they would be annotated and described by a sighted reader for those who are not. Later, I took an exam in Braille set up by the RNIB and passed. Many people outside think prisoners take up education and subjects such as braille in an effort to get parole or be viewed in a good light by those in authority. This is very unjust as I know that most prisoners become involved purely to relieve the boredom and pass their days doing something slightly more interesting than the usual prison options. Personally, I feel there can be few worse breaks in life than to be born or become blind. Involving myself in braille also helped bring a sense of proportion to my own life: whenever I was inclined to feel sorry for myself, just sitting at the machine made me feel pretty glad I was doing the braille and not receiving it. The saying, 'There's always someone worse off than you' is bloody true. I had only to look round me on the wing to see that.

Even though I was the longest-serving inmate there and many felt it was unjust for me to be held in such cramped conditions for that length of time, I felt that I was luckier than most. I didn't have a husband, house and children to worry about, I had good and generous friends who had stuck with me all those years and I had my parents who came to visit me as often as they could. Although every inmate was allowed a visit once every two weeks, my parents could only visit every few months. Apart from the problem of distance and the fact that both were not as young as they'd like to be, visits for them were a considerable expense and meant constant scrimping and saving. Visitors are allowed to bring books, clothes, tapes and so on and to hand over money for an inmate's 'private spends' and this was expense they could ill afford.

However, some inmates came from far across the country and received few visits, and others had no family or friends, which meant no 'private spends', leaving them to rely on their ludicrously small 'wage' to buy some little luxury like a tin of talcum powder. There were also the few who had been abandoned by their families. In some families there is a sense of shame if one member is banged up, whatever they are alleged to have done, so it's not surprising that some inmates are 'hidden'. Maybe their families say that they've emigrated to New Zealand . . . maybe the families emigrate to New Zealand . . . People are seldom perfect.

I looked forward to my visits enormously but was glad in a way that I didn't get visits every fortnight: prison is hardly a good place for conversation, being 99 per cent routine and mediocrity. We'd sit and talk for a while and I'd say everything was fine. I must have said this so many times. According to my mother, I always said it and made light of the situation – and I thought for all those years she had really believed me when I said everything was fine!

Because of the change in Home Office policy in 1984 I was allowed to write letters to anyone I wished, without restriction. This was a big step for me: in relation to my case, many people wrote letters of support and concern. Publicity was growing about the Birmingham six, Guildford four and the Maguires. I had a solicitor working on my case, Alastair

Logan, who was Anne Maguire's solicitor and who had asked to represent me to try and get me an appeal. Support groups were being formed and at last things looked as if they might be moving in the right direction.

I had also for the last few years been writing short stories about incidents in prison and from my life before arrest. A couple of years earlier, a resident writer came to H Wing. This was Tom Hadaway, a well-known playwright in the North-East. He came once a week and a few of us went to his workshops. He told us of his writings, and read ours. He was a real help and encouraged me to put pen to paper about my experiences. When his contract finished, he continued to visit me and write letters, and we are friends to this day.

Around 1986, we were allowed to have budgies, which had long been allowed in the male and some of the female prisons. H Wing seemed to have an aversion to budgies: for reasons of health and hygiene, they said, although what threat a budgie could pose when the sluices regularly over-flowed next to our dining area, I couldn't quite fathom. I didn't really want one at first but eventually I thought it wasn't a bad idea, and Tom bought me one. I called him Mr Chips. Chippy was very far from being a feathered reincarnation of the gentle schoolmaster. He was grey-black with a smattering of white, very large for a budgie and absolutely manic. He had a disconcerting habit of perching on his cage and flexing his wings when people came into the cell; he would then fix them with an evil eye and fly straight at their heads. It's difficult trying to keep up a conversation with someone who is constantly ducking. He was extremely noisy and loved pop music. When I stuck on a Michael Jackson tape he would bounce his head in time to the music and sing loudly, mesmerised, giving a reproachful squawk at the end of the tape. Chippy was great company and rarely in his cage, preferring to fly round and investigate the cell. He had a particular liking for paper. If I was writing a letter he would chew all round the edges. Cigarette papers were another great love of his and I had to be careful when smoking as he tried to take what he thought was a roll of paper out of my mouth. Tom said he had bought him from a shop, but I often thought the shop might have paid Tom to take him away!

Without Tom's encouragement in those years, I doubt I would be writing this book or have shared his enthusiasm for the written word. He visited other prisons in the area and in late 1987 wrote a play which was performed in the Live Theatre in Newcastle. Entitled *Yesterday's Children*, it is based on his experiences of prison and those of the inmates he met. I, of course, was not allowed out to see the play, but watched a video of it and thought it was one of the best plays about inmates and their experiences I've ever seen. Through Tom, I also made contact with some of the actresses in the play, one of whom, Eve, I'm still in touch with; she has remained a good friend.

By now I was also in contact with Michael Farrell, an Irish journalist, who had long been interested in my case. He carried out some extraordinary work on my behalf and did much to focus public awareness on my situation: a great and good man. Sister Sarah Clarke was another great supporter. She wrote to me constantly and spoke out on my behalf whenever necessary. An elderly nun, she has worked with courage and bravery for many years supporting the cause of the unjustly imprisoned. These and many others gave me enormous hope and support through those last few years before my final journey to the Appeal Court.

By the middle of May 1988 I was becomingly increasingly frustrated that nothing had been said about my moving on to another prison. I had driven the senior staff on the wing to distraction, and they themselves had no idea why my transfer was taking so long. Eventually the Governor called me to his office and informed me there had been some delay because of a problem with Cookham Wood staff. Apparently an officer there had been putting it about that she had known me during my short sojourn in the army, that I had known her and her family very well and that she was frightened of me going to Cookham and recognising her, thereby placing her in a difficult position. I couldn't believe it. I was so close to actually getting out of Durham and was shattered to realise that I might be there for another few years. I wrote to my friends outside, who in turn wrote to the Home Office and complained. I was furious, hurt and frustrated like a child whose toy had been taken. I wanted to shout and scream and throw myself down on the floor. My anger was mainly directed at the Home Office, who had kept this information under wraps for months while I was stewing in impatience waiting to be transferred. I strode round the wing for days in a cloud of heavy emotion, avoiding people, unable to talk in my disbelief. I knew it would be relatively easy to check this woman's story as my time in the army had been short. I was told her name and knew instantly that what she was saying was wrong. I had had one very good friend in my army days and had visited her family, but she was not this woman. I asked the Governor to request a check-up of her story by the Home Office. Why they hadn't done this in the first place, I'll never know. They probably assumed that she wasn't making it all up. I gave the Home Office all the information I could about the woman I had known.

A month or so later I was told that I would be going to Cookham Wood and that the officer in question had been transferred to another prison. I enquired whether they had ascertained the truth or not of what this woman had been saying, but I was never told the result of their enquiries, only that it was all sorted out and I would be off to Cookham in a few weeks. Little did I know the furore that had erupted in Cookham over this officer's transfer. The Home Office told me nothing and unbeknownst to me, I was more or less walking into the lion's den.

I suppose I should have realised that we were not all going to live happily ever after, but I was so excited about getting out of Durham, I put the whole incident to the back of my mind. Like a pensioner waiting to be taken on an excursion my bags had been packed for days with a few sets of clothes, cosmetics, books, tapes, radio and budgie. I wrote to friends and family telling them I would be moving soon, I wasn't sure what date. Some of my friends on the wing clubbed together and organised a small farewell party. We had cakes, biscuits and pop and sat and reminisced on our shared past and wondered about the future. It was a great time for me, but I was also very sad to be leaving behind those women who had become friends over the years. I knew I would miss them, even those who begrudged my leaving. It was nothing personal but some of them just couldn't cope with the thought of being left behind; it was too painful for them to contemplate someone else's steps towards the light. I would even miss some of the staff: I had been in Durham for almost fourteen years and some of the staff had been there nearly all the time. We had formed a weird relationship based on forced companionship. I was not sorry to be leaving Durham – I was looking forward to integral sanitation in the cells and lots of fresh air.

On 19 July 1988 I walked out of Durham's door, for the last time, I hoped. People talk about their great journeys: crossing the Atlantic in a tiny sailing boat, walking the length of the Great Wall of China, the Orient Express. This journey from Durham to Cookham was mine. Apart from going out to the hospital some years earlier (and those circumstances were rather different), this was the first time in thirteen and a half years I had travelled any distance from Durham. We travelled in a van with ordinary glass windows, rather than the opaque type which I had been used to for so long. Now that I was decategorised I was awarded the small privilege of viewing the world through clear glass. There were three female officers and a male van driver, the atmosphere was good and we chatted amiably. I was like any rubber-necking tourist in a strange land, soaking up the scenery. I felt a pleasant agony to see people walking past, free, not two yards away, hills, trees, fields and flowers in abundance, I felt part of them, yet apart. Women shopping, kids dragging behind, men clutching babies. Two kids in the back of a car, playing cards. Old people sitting in the sun. A farmer ploughing his land, perched like a lord on his tractor seat.

Finally we arrived at Cookham Wood which, I later found out, was seething with anticipation of my arrival. Its name makes it sound idyllic, redolent of swans on the river, the regal swan-upping ritual and leafy glades. It turned out, for me, about as idyllic as being trapped inside one of Stanley Spencer's more disturbing pictures. As we arrived quite late in the evening, the formality of listing of property was left until the following day. I took what I needed for the night, and Chippy, and was led to my cell. My first impressions of the place were euphoric. Each cell had its own bathroom with a basin and toilet, access to which was through a door in the side of the cell. It is nearly impossible to describe how heavenly and luxurious this felt: I wanted to pee every five minutes and run the taps all day. The restoration of these vital symbols of privacy and liberty boded well for other freedoms. Some of the cells had bunk beds, holding two inmates. I had a single bed. The windows were plastic interwoven with metal strips, but although much larger than those at Durham, they did not let in much light, being scratched and smeared. The door was the same as any cell door: heavy and reinforced metal, a long horizontal strip in place of the usual spyhole; this had a flap on the outside which covered the strip at night time. The cell itself was much larger than any of those at Durham, with walls of rough brick, painted in bright colours. There was a table and chair, wardrobe and a small locker, complete with key, to store valuables in. It was quite a novelty for me to have a key, never mind a personal and private storage space, and I've often wondered why this concession isn't available in every prison. Apparently there was quite a lot of stealing from inmates' cells at Cookham; this had never been a great problem in Durham, although it did occur from time to time. The poor wages and lack of private cash often induced inmates to steal from each other, a practice much abhorred by most of the inmates.

Whilst I was sorting out my bits and pieces for the night, an officer came along and asked if I wanted to go outside. I was startled – it was 6 p.m. and I could go outside! She explained that in summer they often allow the inmates out into the garden. I followed her along the corridor and stepped out into a warm July evening. Some women were walking around a tarmac area, others were lying on the lawn. My eyes lit upon flowerbeds, full of reds, yellows and blues. The fragrance of the grass and flowers made me dizzy with pleasure. It was glorious; a large tree was right in the middle of the lawn, I walked up to it and hugged it. The pleasure and bliss I experienced at that moment was unimaginably painful.

There were two wings at Cookham, north and south, each holding around 125 inmates. My cell was on North Wing. The next day I went through all the formalities of the new inmate. Property was listed and clothes sorted out, then a visit to the doctor, who gives the all-clear, or not, on your health and states what number labour you are. There are different levels of labour in prison. Labour 1 means you're fighting fit and ready for any grot job the system throws at you. The majority of inmates are Class 1. Labour 2 means light work, no scrubbing or lifting, usually applied when you're hospitalised for some reason or, as I had been when recuperating from a hysterectomy. Labour 3 means you're totally useless and fit for nothing except wandering around the place annoying people, usually the staff, who prefer everyone to be Class 1. Inmates who have reached retiring age, of which there are quite a few, are not required to work, but many choose to: not only does it pass the hours, but you don't get paid if you don't work. I was classed Labour 1, which was just as well. I was going to need to be fit for all the hassle that was to come.

The food at Cookham was fantastic. After Durham it tasted like *haute cuisine*: fresh, carefully prepared and presented, delicious and varied. You could actually identify what you were eating instead of being confronted with a mound of evil-tasting unrecognisable sludge. If it's possible to provide such nice food in prison, why can't it always be like this? I speculated on the nasty possibility that time and trouble is taken elsewhere to make prison food deliberately foul, part of the punishment, perhaps. There was the added bonus that the kitchen workers didn't mind if you suggested they could perhaps make bread and butter pudding some time. They were always open to suggestions and tried to provide dishes favoured by the inmates.

Certainly my early reactions to Cookham were mainly positive. I soon learnt that, like Durham, heating arrangements left something to be desired. Prisoners could not control the heating in their cells, so it was too cold at times, but in the main I was quite content. It has to be remembered, however, that I arrived at Cookham in the midst of a simmering disquiet and it wasn't long before the honeymoon – as in the nature of the beast – was over.

A couple of days after arriving, my probation officer, Peter, arrived to see me; he had other clients in Cookham too. He asked how I was settling down after all the recent fuss over the officer. I replied it wasn't too bad. He told me that he had heard that one of his clients, a woman who had been at Durham for some years, had somehow become involved in the situation regarding the officer who had been transferred and stated to the staff that she was now afraid I might be a threat to her. I was nonplussed: I had known her quite well and, although we hadn't been bosom mates, felt that we had got on OK. I was horrified to discover later that this inmate, Debbie, with whom I had been friendly in Durham and to whom I told much of my background, had apparently fed information regarding my army days to this officer, whom she had liked extremely well and who was Debbie's personal officer. Debbie, with other lifers who had also spent time in Durham, had spread tales about me when she heard I was coming to Cookham Wood, in the hope I would not be transferred. So a reputation had preceded me – I was viewed by the lifers and some of the staff as an *agent provocateur*. I was at a loss to understand why these inmates felt it necessary to do this: was I such a threat to them? I had never mixed much with other lifers, preferring the more lively sentenced inmates. Many lifers quickly became institutionalised and knew I despised their defeatist attitude. There is always a coven of bitter lifers who take no pleasure in that of others. I decided not to challenge Debbie on this information; I didn't want to fall into the trap they had set for me.

The TV rooms in Cookham were large and noisy. Not only did you watch TV there, you also did ironing, wrote letters, chatted to mates and generally created a hubbub. It was chaotic at times and I spent little time in these 'association rooms'. I was told about the lifers' room, a small room set aside for the lifers' exclusive use. This contained a few easy chairs, a sort of coffee table and an old black-and-white TV set; there was also a kettle for boiling water to fill flasks. Hot water for drinks was only available from the kitchen at meal times, so if you wanted a hot drink during evening association and had already used the water in your flask, well, you went without. If you were a lifer, however, you could fill your flask in the lifers' room at any time.

One evening I went to fill my flask and took my friends' flasks too. In the middle of boiling the water another lifer came and asked what I was doing. I replied that I thought it was quite obvious that I was filling flasks. She said that it was the lifers' kettle and wasn't to be used for the rest of the inmates. I couldn't believe she was serious, and laughed at her. Immediately she got on her high horse and said she would report me to the staff. I replied she could: 'Fuck off and do it, the water's free and the electricity bill paid by the Home Office, so what are you worrying about?' She left in a great huff; I continued filling the flasks. When I came out, I was pulled into the staff office. She had indeed told the officers and I was given a dressing-down; not that it made any difference – I continued to fill flasks for anyone who wanted. It was a fine example of the policy at Cookham, whether official or unofficial, of divide and rule. Many inmates serving determinate sentences were inclined to think that the lifers were given special treatment and more privileges; in effect, as one inmate put it, 'Commit a murder and you're given star treatment.'

Who could blame some of them for feeling this way? If you were a lifer or long-term-sentence inmate, you were allowed to have rugs, bedspreads and curtains. If you were a short-termer, none of these 'privileges' were available. I found this notion of group preference shocking and felt it was well out of order. In Durham, bad as it was, every inmate, regardless of length of sentence, had the same privileges.

At Cookham association time was another area of dissent. During the dinner period, everybody was locked in. Every other evening after tea there was lock-in until around 6 p.m., when we were allowed out for association until 8 p.m. Otherwise, we were locked in from teatime until the following morning. At weekends, we were locked in from around 11 a.m., only getting out for meal times, so any extra association time given was a big issue. Shortly after I arrived, the Governor called a meeting of all the lifers in our rooms. I didn't want to go, but my friend Lorna (who had moved from Durham to Cookham some months earlier), asked me to. Many lifers were complaining that they didn't get enough association. The Governor informed us that, from now on, we would be having association every evening. Most seemed quite satisfied with this. Lorna and I, however, were not. I asked the Governor if it meant everyone in the prison would receive evening association, he replied it was only the lifers. I was perplexed: the staff said they were trying to encourage lifers and the other inmates to co-operate with each other more, but this decision would only cause further animosity from the rest of the inmates towards lifers. I put this to the Governor, who clearly didn't want to know and, having made the decision, was not open to criticism or further discussion. So most of the inmates were locked up every other evening, whilst a few lifers were allowed to wander at will.

Apart from the dissent it would cause, I didn't want to be out when the rest were locked up. It was like being in a ghost town, no one to talk to but the other lifers. No thanks, mate. I decided to stay in my cell on the nights we were allowed out, with just my friend, Sylvie, for company. If there was no evening association, inmates could have others in their cell until around 7.45 p.m., bang-up time.

Sylvie was in her mid-thirties and, like me, a mouthy little sod. She was serving eighteen months for drugs. Her sentence, in comparison to mine, was 'bed and breakfast'. She had led a travelled and adventurous life and I spent many hours fascinated by her tales. We would play cards, or chat. I still had the budgie, Chippy, then. Sylvie would be highly embarrassed to note that Chippy, having matured considerably, had discovered sex and would often spend frantic moments trying to copulate with a pen! This was sometimes funny but could be extremely annoying when I was trying to write a letter! Sylvie and I kept in touch after her release. She is now beginning to write of her experiences in prison and her life beforehand. Many people find it strange that we enjoyed each other's company, because of the difference in sentence. Every inmate has a unique life in prison and it was useful for us to compare our, very different, experiences.

In any prison there is also a hierarchy of crime, with lifers usually at the top of the tree, gaining an oblique form of respect because of the length of their sentence. I hope I don't sound too big-headed when I say that I was quite popular in Durham and usually got on with the majority of inmates and staff. This reputation was seen as a threat by lifers in Cookham. At Durham, as I said earlier, I and a few friends had been involved in livening the wing up, whether by legal or illegal means. We never harmed anyone and reacted more out of boredom and frustration than malice, but many of the lifers felt we were an unsettling influence and probably thought that I (and others, like my friend, Lorna) would disrupt their dull but ordered lives. I was amazed and felt pure contempt for their attitude. They were now fearful of me, thinking I knew all about their scare-mongering about me and would exact retribution on them, so much so that the staff were now wary and on the defence, anticipating trouble ahead. Not an ideal situation. I was despondent about what their reaction to me would be.

A couple of days later I was instructed to work in the workshop. The workshop? Hang on a minute, I was told there were more facilities here. I've just spent the better part of fourteen and a half years in Durham's workshop. What about the gardens, working as a hospital or education orderly, in the gym, in admin? How about a job in the kitchens, even bin orderly? Oh no, they said, you can't do any of those, you haven't been here long enough and you're also a lifer and all lifers go to the workshop. I was appalled. Fourteen and a half years isn't long enough for Cookham, years already spent doing time in a dismal workshop didn't count. I wanted to revolt, refuse, yet I went to the workshop, determined to be out at the first opportunity. It was a sign of the staff's attitude towards me. Workshops are very restful for containing people: inmates are locked in them until mealtimes and they provide little scope for *agents provocateurs*. I was told by another inmate that it was a test to see how I would react. If I kicked up a fuss, they would tell the Home Office that I was 'difficult' and get me transferred out. So I zipped my lip and meekly put up with it.

It was in fact the very reputation that I had acquired before arriving at Cookham that helped me to get out of the workshop. We had been working on kitchen whites, that is jackets and trousers for inmates employed in the kitchens. A few weeks later a consignment of dark blue material arrived. I asked what we would be making from this material, already sensing it was to do with officers. On being informed that it was indeed for officer's trousers I refused to make them. I was quite happy to do anything for the inmates, but not the officers. It's a punishable offence to refuse to work but I was relying on their awareness of my 'reputation' and the fear that I would spread dissent amongst the ranks of placid machinists who, although they saw my point, were not prepared to put themselves on the line. However, the staff did not know this and it worked. I was transferred out of the workshop and into full-time education. This shows how I learnt to manipulate the fear of the staff by taking control and giving them an unspoken ultimatum: if I refuse, all the others might too, and then their control would be lost. It also illustrates that, even though they might have worked in the system for years they were still ignorant of how inmates would react to a situation. *I* knew before I opened my mouth that few of the other inmates would support me but the staff were unsure, so they gave way and relinquished control.

Full-time education sounds rather grand and liberal, doesn't it? I soon found out that the education department was used as a dustbin for all the misfits, troublemakers and socially dodgy (for instance, those suffering from AIDS). The prison system cannot cope with women considered recalcitrant for one reason or another, who cannot settle into a workshop environment. Many of the instructors refused to have 'problem' women in their workshops. For prison staff who have neither the time nor the inclination to attempt to help these women the education department was the alternative, so the requirement that all inmates should be out of their cells for a given number of hours was fulfilled. Whether they were doing something useful or causing mayhem was not an issue. Women diagnosed as HIV positive or suffering from AIDS were refused access to work areas where there was a possibility that they would have an accident and spread their contaminated blood. It was particularly difficult for them: they were not even allowed to partake in any sports activities and became pariahs, to be avoided at all times. I was sitting next to a woman called Marie one day who offered me a roll-up she had just made. I thanked her and was about to take it when another woman told me that Marie had AIDS and I shouldn't take the roll-up because she had licked the cigarette paper. Marie was upset by this remark and attempted to take the roll-up back. I stuck it in my mouth and lit it and told the other woman she was pathetic and just bloody ignorant and that I probably stood more chance of catching fleas from her unwashed body than AIDS from Marie. The way in which some of the inmates parroted the staff's views on these women infuriated me at times.

I quite liked it in education. There were classes in English, art, home economics, dressmaking and typing. They were quite large, taking maybe twenty women. The English class was chaotic: each inmate on a different level and more or less left to her own devices, and the teacher overwhelmed by trying to handle those who couldn't read or write. There were sessions when we were supposed to do our own studying and although I had the OU course to get on with, it was impossible to concentrate in such an atmosphere. Arguments broke out all the time. Stroppy women quarrelled about who sat where. Others complained they didn't want to sit next to a woman with AIDS, whilst that poor sod tried to regain some dignity in the face of their hostility and ignorance. I attended the art class as much as I could and found a kind of peace in conveying images to paper. The art teacher, Colin, was a born-again Christian. Luckily, he didn't try to convert any of us. I had interesting conversations with him about outside events. We spent hours in furious argument over such issues as Gorbachev and détente, the prison system and Colin's role in it.

After a few weeks I was asked if I wanted to be 'education orderly'. I accepted and found my new 'trusted and responsible' job, as it was patronisingly described to me, to be no more than sweeping and mopping duties. What is 'trusted' about mopping a classroom floor, where all 'dangerous' implements are locked away and the only things of value are some worn-out desks, chairs and cupboards, and even the books are locked away? I spent my days brushing, mopping, making cups of tea and wandering up and down the corridor when I'd finished. Sometimes I sneaked down to the laundry room to see Sylvie, or along to the kitchen where Lorna was working.

Why Lorna worked in the kitchens, I don't know. It must be one of the most underpaid jobs in prison. You have to get up at 6 a.m. and sometimes don't finish until 5 p.m., including at weekends, with very little time off. I would sometimes nip to the door of the kitchen and have a chat with Lorna. We had known each other for years and shared a similar wicked sense of humour, which often got us into trouble but could result in a good laugh. One incident springs to mind.

Two inmates who were new to the prison asked me if I knew who Joan Wright was. Joan was a 'nonce', prison parlance for someone convicted of child abuse and, in prison hierarchy, very low on the ladder. 'Nonces' are regarded as fair game by some inmates and, indeed, by some staff, and are usually protected by segregation. Cookham's policy, however, was to try and integrate them, if possible. The two inmates were youngsters of maybe twenty or twenty-one years and were obviously ready to make a name for themselves. I find physical attacks on other inmates disgusting – the main reason most inmates attack 'nonces' is not because of their crime, however awful and vile it may be, but out of feelings of guilt and insecurity about their own situation. These attacks seem to me reminiscent of the *Gauleiter* social system of Nazi Germany wherein control is enforced by ensuring that however oppressed an individual may feel there is always someone lower down the ladder who can be kicked: 'nonces' are a weak and easy target. It's unfortunate that many inmates don't realise that by taking part in such acts they have already lowered themselves to the very bottom of that ladder. I had long noticed how sad and defeated these women seemed to be. One expects female child abusers to be Cruella de Villes, hard and manic. Yet the majority of those I observed were pathetic and quite beyond the basic self-defence they would have needed on an ordinary wing. In any closed society there will be victims. Although I have nothing whatever to say in defence of women who harm children in any way, their fellow inmates' view of the 'nonces' is interesting in a horrible way, illustrating, perhaps, some of the flaws of the prison system.

I decided to play along with these two youngsters and said that Joan worked in the kitchen and that I would point her out to them. I then rushed along to the kitchen and told

Lorna about them. We decided that Lorna would pretend she was Joan. The two women followed me along to the kitchen where Lorna was in charge of handing out buns filled with synthetic cream. I pointed her out as Joan. The two youngsters were slightly taken aback. Lorna is very pretty and some years younger than Joan. She is also well able to take on any stroppy inmate, or member of staff, for that matter. I introduced 'Joan' to them, indicating they had something to say to her. Lorna placed her hands on her hips, cast an evil eye on them and demanded, in gruff tones, 'What the fuck do you two want?' The situation was not developing as they had envisaged. They had a picture of a quick thump in the gob and kick in the ribs, but now they stood aghast, stuttering slightly in their confusion. 'Joan' got quite carried away in her role, shouted that she knew they thought they could give her a slap and here was something she could give them. She picked up the cream buns and fired them at the two youngsters, who quickly retreated from the dining area under a barrage of synthetic cream and abuse. Later that day they accosted me, saying they had found out it wasn't Joan at all and why did we do it? I just said they had asked the wrong person the wrong question and that I loathed and despised any form of bullying.

One time when my wing was waiting to go to dinner we saw three women attack a 'nonce'. We were standing at the wing door, which was always locked until North Wing had been for dinner. The attack occurred right beside the door. The viciousness of it was disgusting enough, but what was worse was that the officers who were supposed to be escorting her, and protecting her, didn't attempt to intervene. The 'nonce' was carrying her dinner and the women threw it in her face. They then punched and kicked her. It was only after all this that the officers intervened to stop them.

Later that day, I was engaged in my 'trusted' job of mopping the floor of a classroom when the Governor came in. I hadn't had much to do with this man, but from what I'd heard he was arrogant and vindictive and thoroughly unpopular with the women. I told him of the attack earlier and said that I was surprised to see the staff stand by. He got very annoyed and replied to the effect, 'How dare you tell me how to run my prison.' I was quite amazed and told him so. He then stated that I wasn't wanted in this prison and had been foisted on him by the Home Office! I was shocked and said it was OK, I wasn't so keen on being there either, I just wanted to go home. He left in a great huff.

From that day on I began to realise that amongst the lifers and some of the staff there was a concerted effort, quiet but effective, to make life difficult for me. For some months I had ignored the pointed and hostile remarks. A sympathetic officer had pulled me aside shortly after I arrived and told me that I was to be careful: the officer who had left before I arrived had had powerful support from the Prison Officers' Association (POA) and even the Under Home Secretary, and had been extremely popular with certain staff and inmates. My reaction was that it would blow over, the passage of time would dull the situation. In fact, it got worse.

Cell searches were very rare at Cookham; I think I had maybe only one in six months. One morning, though, as I was preparing to go to work, two officers arrived at my door. They told me it was a search so I promptly got my chair and sat outside the cell. It soon became apparent that this was no ordinary search. It took three hours! They not only did the usual clothes and locker search, but turned over and read every postcard, letter and greetings card. Books were minutely inspected – even the budgie's cage got a going-over. I expressed surprise at the length and thoroughness of the search, but was totally ignored. Other inmates passing in the corridor were equally stunned. Some were outraged and became stroppy to the officers. Finally they left, leaving me to clean up and ponder on what the hell was going on; by now I was becoming distinctly paranoid.

The following afternoon we were locked in our cells. It was a Wednesday, when most of the inmates were usually locked in, as the staff held their weekly meetings then. I became aware that more inmates than usual were shouting to each other through the windows. Curious about what had excited their attention I went to mine. I saw numerous members of staff carefully and meticulously searching the grass, the borders, the fire buckets; in fact anything that was searchable

was investigated. I had heard the staff sometimes imple-
mented these searches, mainly for drugs, so took no further
notice.

The next day I was in the art room in education. An inmate
came in and called me to one side. It was Debbie, who had
caused enough trouble already and was now ready to cause a
little more. I had more or less ignored her since arriving at
Cookham and never brought her to task for what she had
said about me. I often thought that not allowing people to
think what they had to say was important was a better
weapon than getting involved in a whole heap of aggrava-
tion. Lofty indifference can infuriate an enemy. Anyway,
here she was, and it was definitely bad news. She had been
in the hospital area on the previous morning and told me that
a gun had been found there. I laughed at her and told her she
was off her head. She then said that word was out that it was
for me! That's why I had got the intensive search and the
officers had been out in the grounds the previous day. I was
flabbergasted, not quite believing any of it; it was like a scene
from a bad black-and-white movie. Debbie also said it was
rumoured that a note had been passed to the staff, anony-
mously, saying that I was preparing an escape. I couldn't
think what to do, so I asked Colin if he had heard anything
about this. He didn't answer – he didn't have to, the down-
cast eyes and slight reddening of his cheeks told me he knew
about it. I marched out of the room and down to the senior
officers' block.

The conversation that followed was unbelievable. I asked if
what Debbie had said was true. The officers, there were two
of them, said no, it wasn't. They intimated, however, that
something was going on and didn't seem at all surprised or
displeased at what Debbie had said. My mind was working
overtime. I wasn't getting any answers here. They wouldn't
discuss anything and gave evasive answers without actually
telling me anything. I walked out no more enlightened than
when I had gone in. I was furious and near to tears at the
whole ludicrous situation. What was I going to do? A decent
officer suggested I speak to the Governor. I agreed.

Later that evening I was called to see the Deputy
Governor. The Governor himself was off at some do or other;

I was quite relieved as I didn't think I would get a sympathetic hearing from him. The Deputy wasn't much better.
It wasn't his fault, he'd only arrived at Cookham some two or
three days earlier and had no idea what was going on. I told
him all I knew and he was at a loss what to say. I stood there
and looked at him and thought, 'What the fuck! They want
you out, so why not give in to them?' Cookham itself was
OK, but the way the place was run left much to be desired.
The situation was definitely getting out of control. The food
was great, but we spent too many hours locked up in our
cells, the whole bloody place was run like a kindergarten,
with none of us being allowed the slightest iota of responsibility. Did I really want to spend God knows how many years
in this situation, constantly worried and viewed with suspi-
cion? It was only a prison after all, and from what I'd seen
not the most enlightened. It wasn't as if I was on the way out
to a real open prison: I could spend years here, any thought
or positive evidence of an appeal were not in the immediate
future. 'Bollocks,' I thought. 'I don't need this. Get yourself
together and take control here.' I told the Governor I *had*
thought of escape, which was quite true; over the years every
inmate does. I didn't bother qualifying this by any explanation. I didn't need to: it was enough. I was locked in my cell
for the night.

The following morning about ten officers came to my cell
loaded with black dustbin liners. They packed my stuff and I
was off – no chance to say cheerio to my mates. Within half
an hour I was on the road to Holloway. I was just glad to be
out of the bloody place and have done with it all. Years later
Sylvie told me they had given her a hard time after I left
because she had been my mate. One officer even told her
they had been informed by someone that I was going to
escape. They had also stated that Sylvie and Lorna were involved too. Whether the gun actually existed at all, or was a
useful fabrication, I have never discovered. If there was a
gun and the staff believed that an escape was imminent, it is
remarkable that I was never punished; nor were Sylvie or
Lorna. There was no investigation and, I was later told,
nothing was ever put in my prison records. It gave me a
small twinge of pleasure to read in one of the tabloids lately,

that Judge Tummin, the Home Office bod who reports on prisons, stated that Cookham Wood's regime had to be changed: there was far too much bang-up and inmates were treated like children.

I was only in Holloway for about three months. I was then returned to Durham before returning to Holloway to wait for my appeal. During that first, brief, period in Holloway I was visited by someone from the Home Office regarding the situation in Cookham. I told him what I thought of it and said that, yes, I had told the Governor I was thinking of escape. I couldn't care less what anyone thought of me, whether I'd handled the situation badly, as he implied, or not. All I knew was that I was the one who had to spend my days there and it's very easy to be critical after the event. He returned a few weeks later, having investigated things for himself. Although he wasn't giving much away, he said that perhaps it was a mistake for me to have been sent there. That was it: discussion now revolved around the immediate future.

I would have liked to remain at Holloway. But it was then basically a remand prison and only took convicted inmates, especially lifers, for up to a month if they needed to be in London for visits from family or solicitor. A new governor had recently arrived there, a liberal man, who wanted to change many aspects of the regime. There were problems with staff, who were resisting such changes. Even though Holloway would eventually take lifers on a more permanent basis, it was decided that Durham was the only place for me at the time. I wasn't entirely happy about this, but there was no choice. I did get a promise from the Governor that I would be returned to Holloway as soon as things settled down.

Nine months after I left Durham, I found myself in a van on the way back. I had mixed feelings about this: frustration that I hadn't stuck it out at Cookham Wood, a calmness and resignation, coupled with despondency due to a niggling thought that the future didn't look good when none of the prisons want you except a top security one, and they only because they have no choice in the matter. By the time I reached Durham in the late afternoon I was thoroughly depressed. Everyone knew I was on the way back, so it was no surprise. Different rumours had reached them through the prison grapevine of the reasons why I was back again. The great escape – I couldn't cope with Cookham – I'd attacked an inmate – I'd been caught actually climbing over the wire fencing of Cookham. I didn't bother to explain. I was sick of having to constantly explain myself, the fact was that I was there and that's that. H Wing seemed so much smaller than I had remembered, there was a claustrophobia about it that really smothered me.

According to the Home Office man, I would be there for about six months. Six months to the Home Office means about a year to you and me. It was in fact thirteen months before I eventually left for Holloway. In the meantime I settled down, finished my OU studies, took the exams and awaited the results with the impatience of any Oxford undergraduate. I had been back in Durham for a few months when I heard some of the most exciting news I'd heard for a long time. During the dinner hour I often listened to *World at One* on Radio 4. I had always felt a need to keep in touch with the outside world, so I listened to the radio a lot in my cell and watched news programmes on TV. I felt it was important to keep up with what was happening; the news often provoked strange reactions in H Wing.

Some news told of unhappy situations. When Lord Louis Mountbatten was killed in a bombing in Ireland years earlier, you would have thought that I, Carole, Anne and the Gillespie sisters had slipped out the night before to do the deed. Inmates were given the day off to watch the funeral. I was amazed by this, and even more to discover that very few, if any, had realised that the same day as Lord Mountbatten died, seventeen soldiers were killed in bombings in Northern Ireland. I'd have thought the inmates would have had more in common with these soldiers than with any minor Royal. My attitude to any pointed remarks that were made through the years over bombing incidents, was: 'Well, if you're so bleeding patriotic, why are you in prison for breaking the law of your lovely country?'

It was in October 1989 when on returning to my cell from the loo I caught the words 'Guildford four'. I turned up the radio and heard that the Guildford four, who were due for their appeal within a few months, were being released in two days' time. I couldn't believe what I was hearing. I ran out of my cell and down to my friends, screaming at them to turn their radios on. We went wild, shouting, crying and laughing all at once. We celebrated with orangeade and crisps which tasted like champagne and caviare to us. On the day they were released we videoed every news report. It was intoxicating and exhilarating and certainly gave me hope that now people would listen and take notice. Although I knew I was still far away from any appeal, that news kept me going for a long time. My correspondence list was growing by the day and I felt more optimistic that my case would be heard. However, as the Birmingham six had their appeal turned down in 1987, I didn't get too excited. Because of the link-up between my case and that of the six, through the forensic evidence of Dr Skuse, I was aware that what happened to them reflected on my case. During those last few months at Durham I became increasingly agitated at not being transferred, especially when I had finished my OU studies and had nothing much to focus my mind on. Luckily the Home Office bod in charge of lifers at that time was more approachable than most of the pin-striped, public school types who'd been assigned before. He seemed genuinely interested in my situation and I had some faith that he'd do what he could to facilitate my transfer. When I wrote to him I knew I was at least addressing a sympathetic face.

Meanwhile work had been started on installing integral sanitation in the cells. The wall into the next wing door was demolished and a new one put up further into the wing, adding ten or twelve more cells to H Wing. These cells were completely refurbished – the work took months, the noise was deafening. A partition was put up between our wing and the new cell area, but it didn't stop the noise or the dust from coming through into our cells and covering our clothes and furniture. Eventually the work was finished and the new cells were given over to the inmates. As you can imagine, there were some real arguments as to who was getting these cells. Who wouldn't want a toilet rather than slop-out?

Those who had been longest on the wing got the new cells. I got one on the top floor in the far corner. It was great: toilet, washbasin and a massive window which opened inwards.

The two long thick strips of metal placed across the window were a definite improvement on the multi-barred and wired old windows. I sat on the window sill for many an hour in the evenings, the view was gorgeous. I could see right over the prison wall to the river and fields, the hills squatting behind protectively. But the pleasure of living in such relatively comfortable surroundings was marred by a very unpleasant and distressing incident.

A friend of mine, Linda, had the cell opposite mine. She was doing a life sentence and was an alcoholic. She had served maybe seven years of her sentence. One bright sunny Sunday afternoon she was sitting on my bed, knitting. She appeared quite content, as much as one can be in prison. We were locked in as usual that night. The following morning she did not respond to the officer who wakes us all at 7 a.m. I heard the constant knocking on her door and the officer's increasingly frantic calls. My spyhole was uncovered and I saw that the officer was beginning to panic: Linda's spyhole was covered from the inside, which was unusual for her. She was usually an early bird. A feeling of dread crept into my stomach as the officer's calls went unanswered.

Some inmates covered their spyholes if they had cut themselves in some way, but I knew Linda wasn't the type to do that. The woman in the cell next to Linda's was banging on her wall and becoming increasingly distressed. The day-shift staff arrived and tried to get a response. Nothing. My spyhole was covered over as were others in the vicinity, and they unlocked Linda's door and went in. I fixed my ear to the door-jamb. When someone had covered their spyhole or refused to respond and there was nothing too much amiss, you could hear the officers talking to the inmate when they had unlocked the door. Now there was a dreadful silence. I craned my neck, hoping to hear one whispered word and somehow I knew that the silence meant there was nothing to say: Linda was dead. We remained locked in for a further couple of hours. The coroner came, the police came, they took Linda's body and, finally, they let us out. I didn't want to leave my cell, didn't want to accept the fact that Linda wasn't there. The woman who lived next to Linda was in pieces; we sat together for a while, not talking, just unbelieving. I wandered downstairs to my other friends' cells.

Everyone was gobsmacked, stunned into silence, apart from distant sobs which echoed round our heads.

It eventually emerged that Linda and a couple of friends had been involved in making a type of 'prison hooch', using fermented fruit. Whether it contributed to her death or not, I don't know. She was due to be transferred to another prison quite soon: maybe she couldn't face the change. Maybe she'd simply had enough of prison and the 'hooch' helped her to do away with herself that much easier. Maybe it was an accident and she didn't really mean to do it. Who knows? All I know is she died. The wing never really seemed the same after that. People often talked about Linda. She was well liked. I was even more relieved to be told I would be off to Holloway quite soon.

10

Holloway 1990

On 12 November 1990 I was transferred to Holloway. Whilst it cannot be said that my eventual and 'permanent' transfer to Holloway signalled an inevitable early finish to my sentence, it definitely boded well for me. I didn't think I would be there for good – even lifers such as I were usually moved once again to an open prison before release – but my previous short stay there made me think that I would enjoy it much more than Durham.

Holloway seemed huge after Durham. People have this idea that it's some Gothic Victorian dustbin with tiny barred windows and cabbage-perfumed corridors. It was once, but the old prison was pulled down and the present one was built on the same site in north London about fifteen years ago. It consists of five floors and holds some 500 inmates. My cell was on the fourth floor, in a wing labelled C4, each wing having its own identifying letter and number. As Holloway had originally been built as a prison hospital, all the cells were large and airy, approximately 10 feet by 16, each with its own basin and loo. There were single, double and dormitory cells, the dorms holding four inmates. We were allowed to put posters on the walls and decorate our cells in our own ways, more so than in either Durham or Cookham. I could see and hear traffic, sense that welcome rumble of a big city on the move, day and night. There was a feeling of bustle and vitality, only yards away.

Even within the prison itself there was an energy very different from that of the small, mostly passive female community in Durham or the ordered, almost stifling atmosphere of Cookham. This was very apparent from the first morning I went to the education department. Around 9 a.m. the doors to the wings were unlocked and we all trooped down the stairs on to a long and winding corridor. Officers were standing at certain sections along the way. Around 300 inmates trooped along this corridor every day, to and from their various workplaces. I discovered this routine was called 'freeflow'. I also discovered that Holloway could have held its own United Nations forum. There were West Indians, Jamaicans, Nigerian, Spanish, Colombian, Hindu, Muslim, French, German and, of course, British women. Freeflow was the place where you met up with your friends who were perhaps on another floor, where news and gossip was exchanged and squabbles and fights began and ended. Because Holloway was mainly a remand prison, freeflow was the place to find out who had got off and who had got sentenced. It was a corridor which turned out an ever-changing and constantly shifting population.

Many women I met were Nigerian, spoke little English and came from small villages in their own country. I felt sorry for them: they had become involved in drugs in order to earn some money for upkeep of their families, and often they lived in poor and substandard conditions. They had been told by the people who sent them that they wouldn't be caught and, if they were, they would be sent home very quickly. So they came, in the belief that they would soon be home with their children but ended up serving ten, twelve maybe fifteen years thousands of miles away from the people they longed to have visit them. It was a desperate situation for them. The problems of culture and language added to their distress, and many were severely depressed. A further problem was the attitude of the Nigerian government, which had been pressured by the British to try and stem the flow of drugs. They decided that after a Nigerian citizen had been convicted in this country for drug-related crimes, and served their sentence here, upon return to Nigeria they would be imprisoned for a further five years as a deterrent. I believe that any person from a foreign country who has been convicted of a drugs-related offence should be deported to their country of origin and their passport impounded. Not only would they be able to enjoy those few privileges of visits, and sustain a relationship with their families, it would save the taxpayers many thousands of pounds.

I acquired a job in the education department. I was surprised to learn that all the teachers were called by their first names, rather than the Miss or Mr employed in Durham and Cookham, where Colin was the only teacher we could address by his Christian name. The teachers regarded all the inmates as adult and mature students, and expected them to act as such. Over the two years I was there, I found them all to be good and sincere friends, people who supported me a great deal. Aided by their encouragement I made great strides in terms of psychological progress towards returning to the outside world. I would like to give special thanks to Richard, Jac, Terry, Hilary, Delia, Carol, Carrie, Ewan and Andrea, to name but a few. As I said earlier, I had already been writing some short stories and other material. Eddie, who dealt with OU courses and some English teaching in general, gave me much sound advice on my writings, many of which are based on events in prison and have been incorporated into this book. He gave special help to me in this and other areas, and has himself already published a novel: *Shambles Corner*. I am pleased to say that I am still in contact with all of these people. This was the first time in my years in prison that I actually did work which I thought could really be 'work' and not just a time-filler of mundane tasks like sweeping and mopping, or mind-numbing machining of trousers.

I worked alongside the civilian clerk, Delia, in the admin. office. Her job, besides the usual clerical duties, involved the listing of all the inmates who studied in the department. Large computer lists were drawn up and needed amending and correcting daily as remand inmates left the prison and new ones arrived. We also had to draw up their wages, which were then taken to the canteen, ready for the next pay-day. Having already worked on computers, I found the BBC computer, on which this information was stored, very ancient and inefficient. The computing world moves quickly and though I had begun my computing experience on the BBC model which is now considered to be almost defunct, I had progressed to the more technological Apple and IBM compatibles. The database program on the BBC, set up by a previous inmate, was beginning to malfunction. After several mishaps, with the machine refusing to print and failing to respond during the filling in of information, I asked the Head of Education, Richard, if we could get another computer. We eventually acquired an IBM compatible one. I transferred all the information on to this, using a spreadsheet program, which gave a much more satisfactory result.

After a few months I was advised to ask for a 'red band'. This is a red piece of material, with one's photograph sewn on and is worn on the arm. It is usually given to inmates who are thought trustworthy and responsible. It was also given to some who were considered disruptive in the hope and expectation that it would encourage them to become more well behaved. I *think* I was given it for the former reason! I was not given the band on first applying for it, though: the Security department, who have the veto on the allotting of bands, tried to block my application, but through the intervention of a senior officer, I did get it soon.

The band allowed me to leave the wing before the 9 a.m. freeflow and walk down to Education through the grounds of the prison. This was quite a pleasant walk, especially during the summer. There were large areas of grass bordered by flowers and quite a few trees, large and leafy. There were also ripped-up sheets, paper, bits of food lying under the windowsills which recalcitrant inmates had thrown out of the windows. Nothing could dispel the pleasure I felt on wandering these areas unchallenged. If one had a band, one had to be early into the department to tidy up before the daily classes began. It was exhilarating and exciting to be allowed to walk freely round the prison: it gave a sense of freedom that I hadn't experienced for a long time, and I used it to the full. One weekend, when it was pouring with rain outside, I put on my coat and my red band and asked the officer to let me out of the wing door. She was surprised, saying how wet it was outside. I replied that I knew and was determined to get soaked. I'm sure she thought I was a bit mad, but I hadn't actually walked in the rain for seventeen years. It was marvellous: I got well and truly drenched and enjoyed every minute of it.

My wages by then were £3.65 a week, and when I got the band they rose to £4.65. This was not because of the band but due to the fact that all redbands work more hours than the rest of the prison population. Most of my wages went on cigarettes.The band also allowed me to stay down in the department during dinnertime and teatime when most of the inmates were locked in while the staff take their meals. I often stayed there, willing to forgo my meals as the food, although different to other prison fare I'd experienced, was not that great. The added bonus was that of choice: I was actually being allowed to make decisions and choose whether I worked over dinner or not. It was all very new and thrilling. However, I was not to be allowed to wear this emblem of trust and independence for long.

I was awaiting the forthcoming appeal of the Birmingham six almost as eagerly as they were. After ten days in court, they were finally released on 14 March. I had been following their progress on TV, but on the day they were released I was working in Education and didn't know they were out until a mob of screaming, excited women arrived for evening classes and told me the news. I was delighted and frantic to see them on the TV. Luckily a friend had videoed the news, and later that evening I watched them step out of the Old Bailey: free men, after sixteen years in prison. I was overcome and cried with happiness for them, even more so when Billy Power stepped forward and asked of the world at large, 'Why is that when we are out, Judy Ward is still in prison?' In that instant, I knew I was going to be out too. Quite when, I wasn't sure, but it wasn't going to be that long. It was like a great weight lifting off me.

On 7 July 1991, it may be remembered, two men held on re-mand for suspected IRA activities produced a gun and made good their escape. What has this to do with me? Well, logically speaking, nothing. I had been banged-up in my cell that night as usual. But logic was never the Home Office's strong point. On 9 July I was working in Education when the Governor arrived in the company of a Home Office bod and they asked to speak to me. This was not looking good. We went into the staff room and they asked if I had heard about the escape of these two men. I was slightly baffled by this question but replied of course, it had been on the news for days. Well, it seemed the incident had spread fear and discord in the Home Office and the Home Secretary had ordered an immediate review of the security in all prisons. So, says I, are you going to build up the walls, install security cameras, ring the place with barbed wire? No, we're taking your red band away! Talk about speechless: I couldn't work out the logic. Would Kenneth Baker sleep easier in his bed, knowing that Judy Ward no longer had a red band? Would this deter future suspects from escaping? I was furious and told them so in no uncertain terms. They assured me that inmates in other prisons had been affected too. Oh, great, is that supposed to make me feel better?

They weren't just taking my red band. That piece of material represented my tiny sense of hope, freedom and independence. Now any small feeling I had that they trusted me had vanished. The staff were at a loss to understand it; some of them couldn't believe it and phoned the security office to confirm what I was saying. The loss of the red band meant my whole lifestyle in Holloway was threatened.

I had recently been moved to D4 Wing. This wing holds about thirteen inmates, and is viewed as a 'privilege' wing. It was ironic in a way that I was moved there. When Holloway was rebuilt some years earlier I had been told that it also contained a new security wing for Cat A females and that I would be moved there shortly. In the event, the idea was scrapped and now I found myself on that very wing, not as a dangerous Cat A but as a trusty redband. The wing regime was very relaxed: we were unlocked from 7 a.m. until 8 p.m. There were no officers staffing the wing; we were trusted to supervise ourselves. We did our own cooking and ate our meals in our cells or seated by the TV and more or less lived as one would in a hostel outside. It was great to live like this after all those years of observation and ordered regimes. To live on this wing, besides being mature in approach, one *had* to have a red band. Suddenly with no red band, I could be removed and placed back in the ordinary routine of the prison. I didn't go to work for a couple of days; depressed and upset by the whole incident, I felt I had lost all the ground I had made since coming to Holloway and was back to square one. However, the officers left me on the wing and, to give them and the education staff credit, they complained to the

Governor about it. I wrote to my solicitor, and to everyone I could think of and they, in turn, wrote to the Home Office and the Governor. Three weeks later I was given the red band back without apology or explanation. Somehow, though, I had lost some of the confidence it had initially brought me and it was a long time before I could even think about the incident without instantly becoming angry. It's a good example of how an inmate may think that they are making progress, when in reality, in the eyes of the Home Office, she is still suspect. It's hardly surprising that inmates have little or no trust in Home Office procedures.

After a few months, the Home Office suddenly decided they wanted Holloway to have an information technology centre, ostensibly for inmates and staff alike to improve and learn the techniques of computing. To this end, they allotted a grant of some £35,000 to the education department. Having by now a good knowledge of desktop publishing (DTP) programs, I asked Richard if I could have two computers and a couple of printers and set up a small DTP business. He agreed. Enlisting the help of two inmates, Anne and Lisa, I installed the equipment in a room which hadn't been used much and turned it into our office. We started on a small scale, producing Christmas and birthday cards, in colour or black and white, and other work units in the prison asked us to make posters and so on for them. The business began to grow and we spent most of the daylight hours in our office, frantically printing out the large numbers of cards, posters, leaflets, pamphlets, brochures and business cards that had been ordered.

Holloway has a lot of visitors, since it is the largest prison for women in the country. The education department also has a reputation for being one of the best in the female prison system. As more visitors saw our work, demand grew. An account was set up in admin. to deal with payments for the orders we were receiving. It was great to work in there all day, knowing that not only was our work appreciated, but we were earning quite a bit too. The money made was put back into the DTP business to buy materials and more hardware. The excitement for us, though, was the fact that we had complete control over the business. We ordered the materials, dealt with the accounts and attended to all the little problems any business outside would have to contend with. There was no interference by the staff, many of whom thought it was a great idea. I'm pleased to say that it is still running with my friend, Anne, now in charge. The business was certainly useful – it helped take my mind off thoughts of appeal, which at the time would have driven me to distraction if I hadn't had the more pressing preoccupations of the business to contend with.

However, I didn't get too involved in the business and found time to join in the other events around me. An actress, Fiona Buffini, came to give drama classes with a view to producing a play. I joined in with the others; there were about eight of us. After months of rehearsing, we put on a performance of Bertolt Brecht's *The Caucasian Chalk Circle*. I enjoyed it tremendously, especially as I was playing Azdak the judge, an irony which was not lost on members of the audience of staff, inmates and outside visitors. Shortly after, we worked with Moira, Fiona's sister, on a performance of Jim Cartwright's *To*, a play about the characters in a northern pub. It was extremely funny and we did a complete send-up of it, much to the audience's delight.

I didn't read as much as I had at other prisons, being far too busy now with the DTP business and rehearsing for the plays. I had no more studies either, which was just as well, as I don't think I would have been able to concentrate properly.

On the second-floor corridor of the department there was a window which stretched from floor to ceiling and looked out on Parkhurst Road. I was told it had been entirely sealed up some time previously. Apparently when it did have an opening at the top, some inmates climbed out and pranced about the adjoining rooftop, shouting to the passers-by below. I used to spend hours looking out of this window. The outside world was only a few feet away: traffic sailed blithely past and pedestrians strolled, perhaps unaware that they were the objects of my curiosity. Some inmates dubbed it 'the wind-up window', but I was entranced to be so near the world at large. Later, I stood there and waved to the members of my support group, who had held their vigils for me outside the prison.

The chairman of the support group was Paul May, who had worked on the Birmingham six case, co-ordinating a campaigning support group. By letter he now offered to do the same for me. Billy Power, recently released, had also offered his support. I sent them a visiting order and a few days later we met. It was great to meet Billy and thank him for focusing attention on my case. The idea of a support group is mainly to bring attention to people's cases and stir public concern and awareness through publicity: for instance, holding vigils outside the prison and the Home Office, printing information on the case and distributing it to the media and public. Benefit nights are held, where people come and have a drink and information is made available about the case, raise funds to support prisoners and offer financial help to their families for visits. There are also regular monthly meetings, which anyone can attend to learn the progress, or not, of the case. People are encouraged to write to the Home Secretary, MPs and so on to voice their concern, and also to the inmate or inmates.

So a support group was formed for me. At first it was strange to have the group offering support, especially financial. Having become greatly independent over the years, it was difficult to accept any form of help. I was also loath to ask for private cash, as I knew that this money had come from the pockets of people who could probably ill afford it. The thought that people had shown their concern by writing to me and attending vigils gave me a great deal more courage to face the seemingly eternal days in prison than any financial boost. I will take this opportunity to thank all the members of my support group for their unstinting and inexhaustible efforts. Those were rewarded when on 17 September 1991 the Home Secretary referred my case to the Court of Appeal. The group had stood vigil for me twice outside Holloway for many cold and bitter hours during some very nasty weather, and it cheered and encouraged me greatly to see them all there, some with babies and young children.

The presence of babies in prison was startling to me. I had heard of the mother and baby units at Holloway and Styal but could never quite imagine what they would be like. The first time I went into the education department I found myself sitting next to a young woman, who had her baby gurgling beside her in a buggy. I just sat there and stared and stared. The art teacher, whose class I was in, noticed me and remarked that it looked as if I had not seen a baby before. I told her it was the first time in seventeen years I'd ever been within touching distance of one. The mother handed the baby to me, I sat her on my lap and examined her as an archaeologist might have looked at a fragment of Egyptian or Chinese pottery. Many mothers came to the department, and there were many babies around. I found the presence of these sometimes smelly and snotty children oddly uplifting. Somehow they made me feel much nearer to the real world outside. If I felt any twinges that my hysterectomy had deprived me of a similar experience, I was still able to enjoy the sight of these young women caring for their children in prison.

I've always felt comfortable around children and can play with them for hours without getting bored and they seem to respond to me, too. Inevitably I think that my inability to have children now has made me especially fond of my nieces, nephews and my friends' children. I try not to think about it too much, because there's no point and it could turn my insides into a bitter little knot, but there are times, of course, when I resent all those lost years. I fiercely regret that my chances of having a marriage and children of my own have been robbed from me. To be honest, I sometimes have to suppress and disguise my fury and jealousy when I am amidst a family – the noise, the comfortable clutter, the evident companionship and the irritating disruptions of the kids. Best not to think about it too much or too often.

Children and female inmates used to cause real embarrassment. There had been a legal loop-hole as long as capital punishment lasted for conviction of certain crimes (as if this was some kind of favour), that pregnant women could not hang because the innocent unborn child should not perish. When Edith Bywaters was hanged in the 1920s – pregnant, but advised not to admit it during her trial as it was thought likely to support the prosecution's case that she was a promiscuous woman – her womb and its contents dropped out as her neck broke. Thereafter, for so long as hanging continued, women went to the scaffold wearing a pair of leak-proof leather knickers so that any nasty mess they made at the moment of death would not spill.

Yes, attitudes towards women who had children or were pregnant whilst on remand had certainly changed by the 1990s. Ruth Ellis, the last British woman to be hanged might have been spared if the jury had known that she was severely depressed and enduring post-abortion miseries at the time of her crime. Nowadays, pregnant mothers in Holloway who have their babies while on remand may keep them with them up to the age of nine months, when they have to be handed out to relatives, or in some cases into the care of the social services. In Styal they allow children to stay with their mothers for up to two years, but it's obviously not an ideal situation for young children to be kept in prison.

Although I found great pleasure and even enjoyment in Holloway, it was not all sweetness and light, happy mums and rosy-cheeked gurgling babies. The last thing I want to suggest is that it was a community of well-adjusted and contented women. On the contrary, many of the inmates were deeply troubled. The majority of women were young and on remand for drug-related offences. There were often scrapes and scuffles, real bloody fights at times. In a place where tensions and frustrations are not easily expressed, a certain amount of squabbling is inevitable and most of the time no real harm is done.

C1 and D1 were the hospital wings which held those considered to be a risk either to the rest of the population or to themselves. Many were women who had tried to mutilate themselves, because of their mental state or because they were 'attention-seekers'. I always thought this description a little heartless: they were obviously drawing attention to themselves because of some profound inner need. Who knows what terrible neglect had reduced them to such desperate acts of mutilation or setting fire to their cells? Very little supportive psychiatric help is available to these women. Living in a prison environment they are expected to conform as much as possible to the ordinary routines, which proves hopeless with some, especially those who are heavily drugged and spend most of the time in total oblivion to their surroundings or companions. These wings were on the ground floor and were very bleak-looking. Most of the inmates spent little time outside their cells. It was often said by other inmates that even the punishment block was preferable to living on C1 and D1. I'm glad to say that in my last few months at Holloway conditions were being improved and attitudes changing regarding the treatment of the mentally ill inmates held there.

The mother and baby unit was far from ideal: it was located on the ground floor where an inordinate number of cockroaches seemed to gather. Arguments abounded over nappy-washing and bottle-feeding. An atmosphere of motherly over-protectiveness was engendered by the reality of caring for a baby in prison. The mothers and babies were eventually resettled in a wing on the fourth floor, one I had inhabited for some months and which was considered to be the best in the prison. It was a definite improvement. Even though we weren't happy to leave our pristine and comfortable quarters for some grotty wing where cleanliness was a dirty word, I think we *all* appreciated that it would be better for the babies.

One aspect of prison life that doesn't change much is visits. Holloway's visiting room was vast in comparison to the others I'd encountered. One could have visits any day of the working week, although weekends were somewhat restricted. One could also ask for a probation visit. This takes place within the probation department inside the prison grounds. Shortly before my parents were due on their first visit I asked if I could have a probation visit, and it was allowed. When my parents arrived, they were met by one of the many probation officers and brought to the department. It was fantastic. We all sat in one of the offices and they were given cups of tea; then we were left alone. My parents were totally overwhelmed by this treatment, having been used to the harsher, over-observed visits in Durham and Cookham. It was the first time in seventeen years that we actually talked, freely and without inhibition. It was fabulous for them, especially. When the visit was ending, the probation officer took them out via the education department so they saw where I worked and met the staff and inmates I worked with. It was great for them to do all this as it not only gave them an idea of what I was doing, but made me feel more relaxed and sure that I was getting on OK.

I had loads of visits whilst I was in Holloway. Most of the friends I'd made over the years now lived in London so it was easy for them to come and see me; they didn't have to book in advance as they had in Durham. Each inmate is allowed to receive twenty-four visits a year and as I had lots of visiting orders saved up over the years I had visits nearly every week.

My correspondence list was growing enormously: it was very unusual if I didn't receive at least two letters a day. Through support group meetings and the production of leaflets containing the facts of my case, which were distributed on a national and international scale, people were becoming more aware of my situation. From these letters I soon discovered that there were individuals who had known for many years, even as early as 1974, that I was innocent but could do little about it until, over the years, public awareness grew and attitudes began to change. Letters were flooding in from all over Britain, Ireland, America, France, Belgium, Holland: I was inundated. Even though I could buy up to sixteen stamps a week, I couldn't possibly have answered all my letters. They were from many types of people – concerned individuals, women's groups, Irish groups, trade union groups and the media. I had received letters from the media for quite some time, ever since 1987 when Peter Gould and Bunty Bax of the BBC started to take an interest in my case. Peter and Bunty often visited me in Holloway and I was introduced to Peter's wife, Julie, with whom I did an extended interview on Channel 4 when I was released. They are concerned and caring individuals with whom I am still in contact and I hope they won't mind me referring to them as friends.

I also had the support of the MPs Chris Mullin and Jeremy Corbyn, both of whom visited and wrote regularly. Here I would like to say thanks to all who wrote to me, and perhaps didn't receive a reply. Believe me when I say your letters gave me great strength at the times when I needed it most. I could ring people too, as phones had recently been installed on most of the wings. We were allowed up to four phone-cards a week, each one costing £2 and holding twenty units. I used the phone a lot to keep in touch with the support group and my solicitor, also to phone my parents. With the money the support group sent me I was able to afford as many pho-necards as I could buy. Although we could phone out, no one could phone in. But the staff at Holloway are much more liberal than those of other prisons and would often accept in-coming calls, and sometimes allow me to take the call myself.

All the letters I received, all the hundreds of Christmas cards, suddenly became more than touching notes of sup-port; they represented my own chance for justice and freedom. Since the release of the Maguires and the quashing of the convictions of the Guildford four, there was a growing loss of public confidence in the police and the judicial system, and a general unease about the integrity and effi-ciency of both.

The forensic evidence of Dr Skuse, so vital to my own con-viction, had now been discredited by the Birmingham six appeal. As he was also one of the forensic experts involved in my case, it followed, logically, that my case might now have to be re-examined. I was, of course, tremendously excited, but still held that niggling doubt. After all, it's one thing to watch the TV and another to believe it could *really* happen to you.

11

Appeal, 1991–92

For some months I had been wondering what, if anything, was happening with my own case. My solicitor, Alastair Logan, had been working on it for some four years now. When he had first taken up my case he was disinclined to seek publicity about it. At that time I was inclined to agree with him, partly because I was worried that fresh press coverage would affect my family and also because of the lack of support for cases such as those of the Guildford four and Birmingham six. However, since the release of the four in 1989, there had been a growing body of support and great publicity regarding the Birmingham six case. I then thought that maybe I should seek publicity, let the media take up my case as they had been requesting for months. Alastair was very reluctant and I was at a loss to understand this. Publicity and support could hardly damage me and I had enough cop on to realise that any chance of release through parole was remote.

When the Birmingham six were released, I became even more concerned that something should now be happening. I felt I wasn't getting anywhere, and Alastair was still tied up with the Maguire inquiry. I had been having sessions with a Dr MacKeith, a forensic psychiatrist, and a Dr Gudjonsson, a psychologist, both of whom had been employed for the defence to ascertain my mental state in 1974, and I felt my appeal could be lodged a little sooner than the 1992 or 1993 that Alastair had suggested.

After a couple of days' thinking about it all I informed Alastair that I would be changing solicitors. Of course, he wasn't very happy, and neither was I. This is not to say that I felt that Alastair was not competent enough; he is a very able solicitor. I changed because I felt a great need for a fresh look to be taken at the whole situation. I contacted Gareth Peirce, whom I had heard of from other inmates and who had worked on the Birmingham six appeal, and she agreed to take on my case. It is right to offer credit to both Alastair and Gareth, both of whom worked on my case without payment. Although I had signed what is termed a 'green form' which would allow for £50 of free legal advice, the majority of work performed for the appeal was done without any payment.

By the end of May the case material had been handed over and I had had my first meeting with Gareth. I knew, after that meeting, that I had done the right thing. Maybe it was because she was a woman, I don't know. I just felt instinctively that she had the situation under control. She has an ability to apply her full concentration to you and your needs and I found her easy to communicate with. She certainly gave me an inner strength with her quiet but determined manner. Within a couple of weeks she had arranged a meeting with some of the Home Office people. They, it appeared, were quite prepared to look over the case, and after some weeks of perusal and consideration they handed it to the then Home Secretary, Kenneth Baker, with a recommendation that it be referred to the Court of Appeal.

The next couple of months were a great strain for me. I was excited at the thought that my case might get to appeal and at the same time worried and anxious in case it didn't. I threw myself into the DTP business with a manic desperation, in the hope that concentration would somehow force me to stop thinking about the matter. A vain hope: although I was able to work for hours at a time without thinking, 'Maybe tomorrow I'll hear something', the ever-increasing amount of mail I received was a heady reminder.

Early on a Tuesday morning I was, as usual, in the education department. I was in the admin. office having a chat when the phone rang: it was one of the junior governors, and she wanted to speak to me. She told me that the Home Office had phoned to say my case was being referred to appeal that day and they wanted me to know before the news was released to the press. I nearly fell down with excitement and relief. I was dizzy with elation, I rushed around the department telling everyone I met; there was great jubilation and congratulations. Immediately I phoned my parents, who were near to tears as I told them the news. Later that day I received a formal notification on paper of the referral. In the months to come, I carried it around with me like a talisman, and have it to this day. An appeal, however, is not a foregone conclusion. Getting the case referred was a giant stride and one which brought freedom that much closer, but just as trials can be politically influenced and outweighed by individuals whose attitude tends to be more than neutral, so, too, can appeals.

Waiting is an agonising process and only the enduring existence of hope can get you through it. When hope goes you might as well be dead and the number of prison suicides and human vegetables bear witness to what can happen when that spark is extinguished. I tried hard not to be too optimistic and held myself in check. Which was quite difficult, when my case had been on TV all day amidst great speculation about the judicial system, and everyone in Holloway was congratulating me. My cheekbones ached for days from continually smiling and laughing.

The next step was for a date to be set for the appeal. After talks with Gareth, we thought it might be early in 1992. It seemed an age away for me, but appeals do take quite a while to prepare: all former trial evidence, if available, has to be gone through and all new evidence to be picked over minutely. The appointing of barristers was also important. We finally decided on Mike Mansfield and Nick Blake, both of whom had had experience of the Birmingham six appeal and others and were well acquainted with the complexities of forensic science.

Mike was a handsome, flamboyant character, clever and witty. Nick was tall, thin and bespectacled with a sly sense of humour and a razor-sharp mind, but it was Gareth who did all the nitty-gritty work. Although they worked as a team, I have always felt that it was Gareth's attention to the *minutiae*, her quiet doggedness and enduring perseverance which finally won my appeal. I heard recently that a film is in production based on one of the Guildford four's experiences, and that Emma Thompson is cast as Gareth. I like the idea that Gareth will get the recognition she deserves, but doubt whether Emma Thompson, award-winning actress as she is, or any other actress for that matter, will be able to portray Gareth's unique character and do her justice. I often think that with 'big name stars' many films produced around prison issues degenerate into glamour and over-dramatisation and so fail to convey the real issues.

The next few months up to that last Christmas, my eighteenth in prison, were a blur of work, visits and letters. Days would go by without a conscious thought of the forthcoming appeal, though it was always lurking in the back of my mind ready to jump forward and distract me in unguarded and quiet moments. Those months seemed to last longer than any of the years I had already spent in prison. Christmas that year became a time of real celebration for me, as if the birth of Christ symbolised my rebirth into society. I didn't take part in any of the dances and events laid on, too impatient in my longing for it to be over. Finally, the New Year bells sang my song of hope. I was entering my nineteenth year in prison. In past years the bells had always been a painful reminder of how long I had been there, but now I compared them with those of 1992 as an art critic would compare a work of Rubens to one by Dali – something new was apparent.

In those first few days of the New Year I was a mass of emotions: happy, bored, frustrated, apathetic, not knowing how to react to each new day, I was exhausted just thinking, 'Will I get a date soon?', 'This time next year, I could be out'. 'But what if they turn down the appeal?', 'When am I going to get a date?' On 10 January I had a visit from Gareth, Mike and Nick and they told me a provisional date had been set for 25 March. Ten weeks – seventy-five days – eighteen hundred hours! I literally began counting time. Slowly I began to feel that nothing in prison mattered any more, I didn't bother rushing off to Education every day, I didn't keep up with my correspondence. Why bother writing letters when you could soon be talking to the people?

On 16 January Gareth told me the appeal court wanted to reschedule the appeal date for the week beginning 9 April. I was furious. It would be after Easter. They're just trying to wind me up, I thought. I was despondent: that was 96 days away instead of 70: was this going to keep happening? Just as I marked up a few days nearer to the date, was it going to be changed yet again? On 5 February Gareth told me the date was now fixed for 27 April: I had to do my recount again – 81 days to countdown. At least it was definite: I was given formal written notification from the Appeal Court. The following day my friends, Anne, Lisa and others, made a large wall calendar with a countdown for 80 days on it. It was a lovely gesture and I was very grateful for their generosity of spirit and support. They had written on the top, 'Countdown for Judy Ward, 19 years too late!'

February 10 was my birthday. The cookery teacher, Olivia, made me a cake and we had a celebration in our DTP office. I received hundreds of cards from people outside, all stressing the fact that it would be my last birthday in prison. I fervently hoped so. The inmates I worked with were particularly supportive because the idea that someone had spent nearly nineteen years in jail and was innocent as well was beyond their comprehension. They admired the fact that I could still laugh and joke and hadn't turned into some kind of walking 'cabbage'. Some inmates were pleased to see anyone released, regardless of the circumstances, because it made them feel that there was still a world outside and gave them a little hope for their own release. The feeling that I was not really part of the prison any more grew stronger from then on. Although I helped out with the DTP whenever there was a rush of orders on, I became increasingly jittery and unsettled. For years I had put 75 per cent of my thoughts into prison and given 25 per cent to the outside world, the 25 per cent representing hope, and now I began to reverse the percentages: it proved a very heady and distracted feeling. I took to going to the canteen to help out there. The canteen, the prison shop, where all inmates spend their wages and private cash, was always busy during the week, and at weekends there was stocktaking and cleaning to be done. I alternated between working in the education department and the canteen. The staff in both were very understanding and left me to drift around, trying to get through the days where I felt I could. My allotment of visiting orders had now been used up and I was given permission to have extra visiting orders as the appeal drew nearer. Many visitors were from the media: they asked innumerable questions, mainly relating to the original trial, and as I didn't have much re-collection of this, they asked about the forthcoming appeal. I was told not to discuss it and to tell the media to restrain themselves to matters relating to prison, time served, ex-periences gained and position now. I enjoyed meeting people and feel that somehow all the visits I had in those few months helped me considerably to relate to people when I was released.

A few weeks before the appeal date I asked Ian, the hair-dressing teacher, to perm my hair for me. Ian ran a proper hairdressing salon, near to the education department. It was equipped as well as any salon outside. He taught classes in all aspects of hairdressing and inmates could take exams, which would lead to professional diplomas, and, hopefully, a career on release. Mostly you had to pay, from private cash, to get your hair done. Some inmates were invited to have it done for free, being used as guinea-pigs for trainee inmates. Because I did a lot of DTP business for Ian, posters and so on, I always had my hair done free. One of the peculiar aspects of prison life is that of changing your appearance, which is viewed as a punishable offence if it is done without permis-sion. If you wanted to change your hair colour you had to ask permission, or have long hair cut short, or a perm, which might change your appearance radically. The reason for this is security: it wouldn't be much use if an inmate escaped and a photo was issued showing long, blonde hair when just a few weeks earlier she had had it cut short and dyed black. After any radical change of appearance you always had to have a new photo taken for the files. I got my hair permed. I wanted to look respectable for the appeal.

Being at Holloway was a considerable help to me. I had been left to make my own decisions and choices and I had a red band, which allowed me a sort of freedom in the prison. All this and meeting the many visitors who came to Hollo-way were good preparation for coping with life outside. I suppose there are some who would say I rehabilitated myself. I dislike the word 'rehabilitated': it conjures up an image of a caring prison system and the availability of untold facilities all geared to preparing the inmate for the outside world. It's not that I don't think it is useful, but the way it is usually approached is often useless, and sometimes down-right damaging. Most inmates lack the confidence needed to face life in the – possibly much changed – real world. Throughout one's sentence an inmate has to place a great deal of dependence on the system; such is the system that officers have to be asked for even the most basic items. For instance, if you had your period you would have to ask an officer to unlock the store cupboard and give you sanitary protection, as in Durham. Responsibility there for even the most mundane of matters was taken from you. I believe that this dependency contributes greatly to recidivism. The ways in which 'rehabilitation' is applied should be examined more closely; inmates need to be weaned off the dependency of an institutionalised lifestyle. More to the point, it should be done long before they go through the system and arrive at the open prison, as is now the case.

The expectation is that inmates will begin their sentences in secure conditions and, as time progresses and parole dates are reached, they will sent to an open prison. Open prisons offer a lifestyle more in line with that of the outside world, with limited supervision and greater freedoms and privileges than in the more secure establishments. There are work hos-tels, where inmates live and attend jobs in the surrounding towns, returning to the prison at evenings and weekends. In theory it sounds pretty good. In practice, however, it is very different. The inmates are not free and in some ways their lives are made more frustrating by the restrictions that still exist. Whereas most people on the outside can be cheeky now and again, make a personal call on the office phone or slip a few paper clips into their pocket without being fired, if inmates from an open prison do any of these things they can be dismissed, they can be returned to more secure conditions and their parole dates can be put back. Some inmates find it difficult to cope with an open prison after spending years in the more conventional ones, and run off. Some even ask to be returned to conventional prisons. Open prisons usually have market gardens or mini-farms, where vegetables are grown for the prison, and there are often cows or pigs. Although I'm sure it's a very healthy lifestyle, I fail to see what form of 'rehabilitation' this offers to inmates, the majority of whom are 'townies'. It is a working experience that is unlikely to help them after release.

There is, as yet, little psychological counselling; inmates are all too often allowed to wallow in the cliché that it was bad breaks and social disadvantage that got them into prison and all too seldom made to confront the idea that they are responsible for their own actions and any consequences of these. If you consider these factors, combined with a lack of responsibility, great feelings of insecurity and total dependence on the staff for one's every need, it's no surprise to learn that so many inmates return to prison: they haven't a clue and have never been shown how to survive outside the walls. How can inmates be expected to become responsible citizens and take their place in the community, to use the weary old phrase, if they are treated like dangerous children and given no notion of personal responsibility or of what they might achieve in the future? Inmates should be treated as the adults they are, serve their time in more open environments and be encouraged to learn practical and personal skills which will help them to survive outside and not be dragged back to the familiar sound of that turning key.

People usually leave prison exactly the same way as they were when they came in. Even in Holloway, which these days is regarded as a rather enlightened place, the number of recidivists is high. Prince Peter Kropotkin, the Russian anarchist, described prisons as 'the universities of crime'. For most of the inmates, advice on drug-dealing, fraud, blackmail, housebreaking, shoplifting and armed robbery is mostly entertainment for a rainy day and will never be relied upon. After all, if they were so good at it why are they banged-up in the next cell?! Some inmates, though, take the advice because they have no idea of other ways to survive outside. I was lucky in that I actively sought ways to assert myself and achieve some form of independence and self-worth.

As 27 April approached, however, my self-worth was very shaky, my mind in turmoil. Because of the nature of the appeal and the vast amount of information needed for it, I had to relive the events of 1974 for Gareth and others such as

Dr MacKeith and Dr Gudjonsson. I tried my best to remember but the stress associated with that time reasserted itself. I had difficulty sleeping and felt a need to talk over the situation constantly. It must be remembered that much of the evidence gathered for the appeal was totally new to me and I was appalled to learn that if this material had been offered at the time of the trial I would never have been sentenced in the first place. I was angry and felt very bitter as more and more information emerged.

One piece of information I was given bothered me more than most. This was the fact that the Home Office had itself set up three independent reviews into my case, in 1985, 1987 and again in 1989. I knew that the Home Office must have had certain qualms about my case, otherwise they would never have bothered to any review, let alone three. The fact that they never informed me, my solicitor or anyone and had carried out these reviews entirely in secret agitated me to a great degree. It seemed a bitter irony to me that, just before I was decategorised in 1987 and having done one review already, the Home Office informed me it would be bad for me to seek publicity as any adverse attention could affect my decategorisation and transfer from Durham. I, in my ignorance, complied with this 'advice' and I would say to any inmate who is wrongfully imprisoned: seek as much publicity as you can muster and ignore any 'advice' from the Home Office.

My mind was full of questions and doubts, thoughts of the uncertainty of the immediate future exhausted me, yet I couldn't sleep. One moment I was snappy, the next full of hope and expectation. On 2 April Gareth told me that, although the appeal would start on the 27th, we would not be attending until the 29th; the judges wished to go through the material before the actual appeal process started. I started to get a bit paranoid then: 'Is it a ploy so they can turn my appeal down flat as soon as we walk in?' 'Is it good news that they wish to read all before the appeal, or not?' No one knew; we were playing it by ear and hoping for the best. The news did little to settle me and I asked if I could move into a friend's cell so I would at least have someone to talk to during the evenings.

In Holloway, inmates were sometimes allowed to move in with a friend for a while, if they had bad news, or were not feeling very well or were depressed. With four weeks to go to the appeal, I packed my gear and bed and moved in with Iris, a woman the same age as me who was serving nine years for a drug offence. She was mature and wise and funny; we spent hours talking, about ourselves, our families, the appeal, the prison, the inmates. It was a great help to me as well as being highly unusual: it was the first time in nearly eighteen and a half years that I shared a room with anyone. I think I drove Iris round the bend, and she would often curse me, with a rich cockney twang, for keeping her awake when she wanted to sleep. However, I too remember nights when, just as I was about to sleep, she would spring up in the bed and shout across to me, 'Ere Jude, did I ever tell you . . . '.

By 27 April I'd packed all my gear, left instructions with Iris what to do with various items I was going to leave behind, had had what I hoped would be my last visits and had written my last letters. I was wondering whether the judges were reading the material and, if so, what they were thinking, when I was called for a visit. It was Gareth. It was bad news. The prosecution had stated that they were going to ask for a three-month delay when we got to court on the Wednesday; they said they weren't prepared. How could they not be prepared? They'd had the same time as the defence to prepare, and we were ready. Edvard Munch must have painted *The Scream* with me in mind, because that's exactly how I felt. I couldn't get through another three months of this, I was mentally exhausted as it was. One can cope again and again, but there comes a time when your inner resources are about to fail you: it was that time for me. What was I going to do? I quickly ran and phoned Billy Power, so he could spread the news. Fortunately, he and Paul May, the chairman of my support group, were on their way to a press conference.

The next day there was great publicity on TV, radio and in the newspapers. Many people couldn't believe that this could happen when we had got so close. My defence team were ready to fight it. Later the same day, I was called to speak to one of the junior governors. The Home Office had contacted the prison and told them I could no longer phone any of the media and that if I attempted to do so it would be viewed as a punishable offence! The reason for this was that the prosecution had complained about the amount of publicity over their plans to delay. I laughed and said that as the press had already printed and I was going to the Appeal Court the next day, there was no one I needed to phone. I realised then that a fight was beginning. In some way this strengthened my resolve, and I gathered my last shred of resources together in preparation for the final fight, as I saw it.

On Wednesday, 29 April I travelled to the Appeal Court on the Strand. I had been woken early to get ready. Wearing a new trouser suit my support group had sent me, I climbed into the van for the short, half-hour journey. I noticed little about the streets through which we passed, or the people, my concentration locked into the coming conflict. Around 10.15 a.m. I climbed the steps into Court No. 4, accompanied by three prison officers. The appellant's seat was in the near left corner of the room. On my left and facing the court was the judge's bench, opposite me, the witness-box; below me and to the right my defence were seated, nearest to me and beyond them, the prosecution. The back of the court was for spectators. The court was full, I saw familiar faces: Michael Farrell, Billy Power, Paul May, Chris Mullin, MP, Anne Maguire, members of the media. The atmosphere was tense, it was an important day for all of them there. A slight rustling sound alerted us to the entrance of the three judges. We all rose until they had seated themselves.

Lord Justices Glidewell, Nolan and Steyn nodded to the court. Mike Mansfield rose first and cited the grounds for appeal. Then the prosecution barrister, a Mr Langdale, rose. He gave the reason for asking for permission to delay the appeal: they had no assessment of my mental state in 1974, as had the defence, from Dr MacKeith. They had only just appointed a forensic psychiatrist and they wished to produce an assessment, without which they would be at a disadvantage. While all this was being said I was taking notes, as I did every day until my release. It was just as well that I decided to do this, as I couldn't bear to look at the prosecution and needed something to concentrate my mind on, otherwise I have the distinct feeling I might have jumped up and shouted, 'What a load of bollocks!'

The judges heard the prosecution and then retired to decide what to do. Gareth was a little worried that they might agree. I felt somehow that they might not. I had noticed the judges glancing across at me now and again and, more importantly, Justice Glidewell had twice corrected Mr Langdale when he had mistakenly referred to my 'seventeen years in prison', Justice Glidewell stating that it was eighteen: maybe the two days' reading had not been such a bad idea after all.

The judges returned and spoke for some while about the reasons for the delay. They then informed us that there would be no three-month delay – the case would continue until the evening and then be adjourned until the following Tuesday, giving the prosecution five days for their forensic psychiatrist to visit me. The court erupted, people cheered and clapped, I threw my fist in the air, my relief was such that I could have jumped over the bench and kissed the judges. Justice Glidewell peered over his glasses and said, 'There will be no clapping in the court', although I'm bound to say it was a mild reproof and I think he was probably quite pleased with the reaction. It was a major victory and cheered me up tremendously. The world outside suddenly became nearer than a TV set.

Even at this stage of the appeal it emerged that vital pieces of information had been withheld from my solicitors at trial. All of the prosecution barristers and the various police forces involved, as well as the DPP, had been circulated with medical reports suggesting that I was unfit to plead and had been informed about my attempted suicides whilst on remand. My defence team had never been informed of these reports and the appeal judges were very angry at these continued attempts to cover up. Sometime before the appeal was due to be heard my defence team had requested access to my medical records from 1974. The prosecution stated that they couldn't find them and suggested that perhaps they didn't exist. This was clearly ridiculous as Dr MacKeith had already taken notes from them whilst on a visit to Holloway. Finally they produced a few sheets which included a list of my property and even blank sheets of prison-headed paper. A few days later these reports – which of course were not quite the same thing as medical records – were handed over to the defence having been 'found in an unused cupboard in the prison'.

On a lighter and more ludicrous note one piece of evidence which was never to be heard was that of Brandysnap. 'Brandysnap' was the name of a dog trained to sniff out explosives and the CPS had produced a statement from his trainer to the effect that Brandysnap was one of the best sniffer dogs ever, and if he sniffed out explosives in the caravan I had lived in then he was right. Even the appeal judges were amused enough to comment that they really didn't think it was necessary for Brandysnap to be called to give evidence.

For the next five days I had sessions with Dr Bowden, who had been appointed by the prosecution. It was exhausting, as I had already gone through this type of questioning with Dr MacKeith, but it was something that had to be done.

We returned to court on 5 May. Dr MacKeith had to give evidence first and was quite worried that I might get upset about what he was going to say. I told him I didn't care, he could call me what he liked as long as it wasn't a terrorist. For the next three days all the evidence was related to my mental state in 1974 and beyond. Dr MacKeith and Dr Gudjonsson both made their appearances. On Friday the 8th Dr Bowden was called for the prosecution. After giving evidence, it emerged that he had come to more or less the same result as Dr MacKeith, which was that the statements I had given in 1974 before my trial could only be classed as 'unreliable' due to my state of mind. This was not good news for the prosecution.

At 11.50 a.m. all evidence had been heard. We all sat anxiously on our seats, knowing that something was happening, but not quite sure what. Mr Langdale rose to ask for an adjournment until Monday morning, stating he needed to ask advice from the Director of Public Prosecutions and that they would be conceding the appeal on Ground E, that of unreliability. Their case was falling apart; they were prepared to throw in the towel. I was ecstatic. Justice Glidewell agreed to adjourn the appeal, stating that on Monday morning he wished to be informed as to how long the appeal was likely to last. He wasn't the only one who wanted to know.

Shortly after, I returned to Holloway, where it was quite funny to observe that some members of staff had thought I had already been given bail and were actually debating whether to let me back into the prison. I convinced them that it was only an adjournment and I hadn't got bail and finally managed to get in! I was on tenterhooks all weekend; everyone was saying, 'You'll be going home on Monday.' Although this idea was beautiful to contemplate, I was prepared to wait and find out before believing it completely. On the Sunday, although no legal visits are allowed, Gareth was able to come. She told me that I would probably be getting out on Monday! I was nearly sick with excitement.

On the Monday morning I arrived at the court in a fever of anxiety. Mike, Nick and Gareth came down to see me. Mike said the prosecution had conceded and that I could be released that day. However, if the defence agreed with the prosecution it meant that the evidence relating to non-disclosure of material and forensic science tests might not be heard. The plan was to agree with the prosecution on the conceding of the appeal, but also to ask the judges to carry on the process, so the new evidence could be brought out.

We wanted a number of scientists to give evidence, especially a Mr Higgs, who had been involved in the case of the Maguire family. It would be the first time that evidence of notes concerning experiments of explosive substances performed before my trial in 1974 would be given, and would prove to be highly important. Also, evidence that the DPP at the time had failed to reveal vital witness statements which would have been relevant to the evidence of the bombing. My 1974 defence team had written to ask for disclosure of all statements and had been informed that there were none. There were in fact over ten thousand statements given which showed that others had committed or been involved in bombings with which I had no connection.

Whilst we had the platform and the hour, it was important that the non-disclosure and forensic evidence was heard, not only for my appeal, but for the legal system in general. However, if the judges agreed to hear the rest of the evidence, they might just not release me on that day and I could possibly spend a few more weeks in prison while they heard the rest of the evidence. It was a quandary for me: so near and yet this hiccup meant so far – three weeks seemed a lifetime away. In the end, I thought that as I was still in prison at this stage I could bear it for a few weeks more.

I thought that we would soon find out what the judges were to decide, but it was not to be that soon. Mr Langdale rose at 10.30 a.m. and spoke at some length; in fact, it was 1.10 p.m. before he stopped talking and only then because the judges were becoming impatient as to the point he was trying to make. He was, in fact, trying to stop further evidence being heard, saying that as he'd conceded there was no need for this. Justice Glidewell then adjourned the session until 2.30 p.m. to consider what he had heard.

I paced up and down my little room, wondering if it was going to go on for another day, frantically chain-smoking and feeling sick with nerves. My bottle's going, I need some Valium, I need some brandy, why doesn't someone tell me what's happening! Gareth came down and said it would either finish today or I would get bail. I crossed my fingers and toes as I climbed back up to the court.

Justice Glidewell began to speak, on Ground E, 'unreliability'. The conviction would be quashed but because all the grounds concerning non-disclosure and forensics had not been heard, they could not yet formally quash the conviction but would do so when all the evidence had been given. In the meantime the appellant would be given 'unconditional bail'. I was free! I could go and catch a bus, take a tube, walk in the park, swim in the sea! I was breathless. Justice Glidewell turned to me and asked if I wanted to go down and arrange the bail. I rose and said, calmly and quietly, 'No thank you, Your Honour, I'll do it later', and sat down again. Was I mad? Had the excitement been too much for me? I knew that the appeal had to carry on that day and it was much easier for everyone to carry on for another couple of hours. I continued to take notes, but with far less concentration, glancing around the court at my friends, giving discreet thumbs-up signs.

The court session ended around 4 p.m. I went downstairs

and had to sign all kinds of forms, not knowing or really caring what they were. I was handed a small sum of money, my bus fare, I presumed. I had no belongings, my only clothes the ones I stood up in. A couple of burly policemen escorted me to the entrance door of the court. Crowds of well-wishers and friends surrounded me in a warm and friendly grasp; in a delirious muddle we almost danced to the doorway to the street. I looked out – hundreds of faces looked back, dozens of cameras, the media shouting questions, I couldn't hear what they were saying. I walked, was almost lifted across the pavement to a waiting car. Half-way there I stopped, raised my arm and shouted, 'Eighteen years, three months and five days'. It was enough, the time I had spent waiting for freedom. Gareth and I were bundled into a car and driven to her house. My first action was to phone my parents, I wouldn't let them come to the Appeal Court – the press would have hounded the life out of them – but they came down to London three days later and stayed with a friend.

Later that evening, hordes of people descended on Gareth's house: friends, support group members, staff from Holloway, some of the Birmingham six and their friends and relatives. A great gathering, a blur of kissing, laughing, shouting and hugging and of course, drinking – champagne, wine, in fact anything that was available. At one point I left the house with Billy Power; we went for a walk down the road. It was around 9.30 p.m., I would have been locked up an hour and a half ago, the night before. We went into a shop and I bought a few items: cigarettes, chocolate, silly things, just for the experience of shopping. Billy warned me that for a while now my life belonged to everyone else: everyone would want interviews, everyone would want to talk with me and buy me a drink. I hardly heard him, I was so busy taking in the sights and the experience of walking down a road again. Later that evening a few of us sneaked off to the pub. Leaving the rest to their celebrations, we had our own quiet celebration. It was a great night, I was incredibly happy and I was rat-arsed. I went to bed.

That first morning, waking up on a soft divan bed in a real bedroom, the trees waving at me outside the windows and birds congratulating me with song, I lay and luxuriated in the moment. From now on I would be making my own decisions and choices; the thought was intoxicating. That first morning I accompanied Gareth to the Appeal Court, as we were unsure whether my presence was required or not. When the morning session ended around 1 p.m., Gareth enquired if it was necessary for me to attend. The answer was no, only on the day the appeal ended, when judgment would be given. I would be notified of this date in writing. That was it – I was off; the case could be left in the capable hands of my defence team. Accompanied by Maureen, a young woman who worked in Gareth's office, I decided to go and do some shopping and savour my freedom. Running the gauntlet of the press gathered outside, we jumped in a taxi and headed for Oxford Street. With the money I had been given by the support group, I was able to do some shopping. This was no big spree, I just needed some clothes.

The next few days were busy and vigorous. Every morning on waking, I would languish and snuggle luxuriously in the bed for a while, but the urge to be up and out became overwhelming and I would fairly leap out of the bed in eager anticipation to walk the city. Just going into a shop and buying a few cigarettes, taking a tube or going for a bus ride, walking in Hyde Park for hours, gave me a great thrill and feeling of contentment.

The press were clamouring round. As the appeal was continuing, I was as yet officially unable to give interviews. However, as many promised not to broadcast until after the judgment, I spent quite a few days being driven round from studio to studio. Most interviews consisted of the same old questions: Was I bitter? How did I feel? What was I going to do now? Now and again some journalists asked interesting questions regarding the judicial system and law and order in general. I noted that it was only a Yorkshire TV journalist who asked me about the bombings in 1974 and how I thought the families of the victims killed felt then and now. I replied that they must have been feeling bloody awful. The bombing itself was atrocious. Not only did my release dredge up memories, associations and miseries that they had tried either to forget or to come to terms with, but the establishing of my innocence meant that they could no longer cling to the small compensation that someone had been punished for the bombing. But, I reminded him, I too, was a victim, as were my family. We had all suffered needlessly.

Staying with a friend, my parents were away from the eyes of the press. We spent every day together, walking round London, seeing the sights and enjoying the linked arms and shared happiness. I had terrible trouble convincing my mother that 'unconditional bail' meant I wasn't going back to prison. She had an idea that until the final judgment things could go wrong and she would again find herself visiting me in Holloway. I had to get Gareth to speak to her, which helped somewhat, but she was never completely convinced until the judgment was given and it was all over.

I was finally notified that Thursday, 4 June was the judgment day. The appeal had been heard; what would be interesting now was to hear what the judges had to say about it all. The court was packed. Just before the judges entered, the clerk of the court, a Mr Thompson, approached me and handed over a brown envelope. On opening it I discovered the official quashing of the conviction, which Mr Thompson had had framed for me. I was overwhelmed by his generosity of spirit. I waited for the judges, clasping what represented my vindication. It was a very special moment and I'd like to thank Mr Thompson for his recognition of what it meant to me.

Lord Justice Glidewell read out the judgment. It took nearly two hours to go through. Forensic scientists, police, prosecution lawyers and the prison doctor at Risley were all to blame, he said, having been found guilty of concealing evidence that might have pointed to my innocence. The judges attacked the 'partisan' scientists who conspired to hide material that would have considerably weakened the prosecution case. It was good stuff. I was told that never had the judges so strongly attacked anyone as they did that day. The one phrase that stuck in my mind and provided the title for this book was, 'Our law does not tolerate a conviction to be secured by ambush.' More importantly, they set out a series of guidelines, warnings and markers for the judicial system in general, stating that, above all, the prosecution had a duty to alert the defence to all evidence it had obtained.

In most trials the prosecution has untold resources available to gather information. In some cases, material gathered was not always made available to the defence and the prosecution, in order to secure a conviction, had not felt obliged to hand it over. As most defences are run on legal aid, not only does the defence lack the resources of the prosecution, it is also unaware of material which could affect the outcome of the trial. In a land where every man and woman is regarded as equal, the judicial system seems to consider that some are more equal than others. Ideally, my judgment would have some effect on future trials. In the Matrix Churchill case, for instance, the defence used my judgment to request of the judge that the prosecution hand over material which, in effect, saved Paul Henderson and others from going to prison. I'm glad that my judgment is now being used in courts: it is a small compensation for the years in prison. There is still far too great an imbalance in the judicial system, with the resources available for prosecution far outweighing those of the defence. The term 'a fair trial' means little whilst this imbalance exists.

The judges finished reading, stating they 'greatly regretted' my being convicted. I left the court, clutching my official notice of acquittal and a large bunch of flowers someone had thrust into my hand. It was less euphoric and exhilarating than the day I received bail, more a joyful acceptance. It was the first day of the rest of my life and I felt a quiet satisfaction. That night we had a great rave-up at the Irish Centre in Camden with friends, supporters and the defence team. I drank and danced, it was a celebration of freedom.

12

Freedom

I stayed on at Gareth's for some four months, while I searched for a flat and began to adjust to life on the outside. As I began the processes of acquiring everyday items such as passport and bank account I realised I was, in some way, without identity: much like the 'Invisible Man', I had disappeared off the face of the earth. For example, when I went to a bank to open an account I was told I needed some form of identification – a gas bill, poll tax form etc. I replied I didn't have any of these items. I was asked my address and gave Gareth's; when they learnt that I had been there only a few weeks I was asked for my previous address. I was greatly amused, on giving HMP Holloway, to be asked if this was a private address! I finally got the account after some explanation and embarrassment on the part of the young man asking the questions.

Travelling round London I was occasionally recognised. People stopped and congratulated me and wished me luck for the future. One incident I will always remember. I had taken a taxi to meet a journalist for an interview. The cabbie recognised me and we chatted amiably; on reaching my destination he refused to accept payment. I tried to insist, but he drove off with a cheery wave. It was a lovely gesture and an example of how some people acknowledged the injustice of my past situation.

I spent some days looking over different flats before I found the one I now live in. It is near to one of London's parks, in a large 1930s purpose-built block, on the second floor. It's not very large but it suits me well: living-room, bedroom, kitchen and bathroom. I chose it mainly because it had recently been decorated and most of the furniture, plus fridge, cooker and washing machine, was included in the selling price. I have little interest in fretting about colour schemes or shopping for furniture, so I considered it well worth the money. With the interim payment of compensation received from the Home Office I paid half the price of the flat and secured a mortgage for the rest. There has been great speculation in the press about how large an amount the compensation will be. I have, as yet, no knowledge of the final amount; the Home Office has given only one interim payment. However large it may be, it can never make up for the deprivation of all those liberties which people outside have enjoyed, probably without even being aware they are enjoying them.

While the paperwork was being done on the flat I decided to go to France. My elder brother, Eric, had phoned me to say he was going over in the car and asked if I wanted to go. Having never been to France, I was delighted. My brother is mad about the Tour de France and cycling in general; he was taking his racing bike with the hope of cycling on some of the routes the Tour de France had covered. I travelled to Newhaven and met Eric on the ferry. It was quite an experience for us both. We hadn't met, except once, for about twenty-five years and at first our relationship was a bit strained. As the days passed, though, we soon discovered that in some ways we had a lot in common and spent many hours discussing our lives, our family and the world in general. We had both left home quite early in an urge to seek pastures new and escape the grim monotony of a grey northern town. We had both studied with the Open University; in fact we had both, more or less, covered the same courses. As we drove across France in a hot July, I delighted in discovering the beauties of the Dordogne and the Loire. Rugged mountains, medieval villages, rolling hills and wide, smooth-flowing rivers shaped my prison daydreams into reality. It was gorgeous and I loved every minute of it. Sometimes I wandered round the villages, taking in the sights and characters. Here I was unrecognised and it was nice to be regarded as just another rubber-necking tourist. Other times I did nothing, just lay and revelled in the sunshine and my freedom.

Eric passed most of his days cycling up mountains. I thought he was quite mad, especially when, at the end of the day, he returned exhausted and burnt by the sun. In the evenings we would find a restaurant and try out the local delicacies, then stroll along wrapped in the velvet warmth of the summer nights, stopping occasionally to take a cool drink and observe with idle curiosity those around us. It was sheer bliss and I returned to London bearing fond memories and many photographs and a realisation that I quite liked this 'new-found' brother.

I have been to France twice since then, both times to Paris. The first time I took my parents and we stayed in the Hilton for a week to treat them to a taste of luxury. It was something I had always been determined to do. It was, as my mother put it, the holiday of a lifetime. The second time I went with Sylvie and this time we stayed equally happily in an ordinary bed and breakfast place, being used to less pampered surroundings! I have also been over to Ireland three or four times, to say thanks to the people over there, in both North and South, for their support during my years banged up.

Freedom after years of incarceration can be a heady and exhilarating feeling. People want to celebrate by plying you with drinks, inviting you to parties and pubs and generally rejoicing in your freedom and their relief after a hard-won fight, usually over many years, to secure your release. It is understandable that one goes on a 'bender' now and again. However there is a danger here too: one's life can become a non-stop celebration, which in some ways can prevent one from adjusting to the more normal routines of society. I was invited to Dublin to celebrate the granting of a pardon to Nicky Kelly by the President of Ireland. Nicky had been accused of a mail-train robbery and was unjustly imprisoned for some years. The party was attended by crowds of people, amongst whom were Billy Power and other members of the Birmingham six and their relatives. The party began on a Friday night and continued through until the following Sunday, with breaks for sleep and food as the party moved round from hotel to pub and back again. It was the first real bender I had been on and it exhausted me. I wasn't used to alcohol and the lack of sleep, and was somewhat relieved to leave them on the Sunday morning. It was a great party and we had a really glorious time and lots of fun but I knew I couldn't keep up the pace.

A footnote to this is the recollection of Billy Power saying to me at one stage, 'Don't get on this train, Judy. People will want you to go everywhere, to give talks and attend meetings and celebrate. Find your own place and your own space, step back and take a breath and hold on to your privacy.' He was in no way condemning anyone, just stating a sad fact that if you continue to live in celebration after release any sense of stability may be lost. Of course, people will always want to slap you on the back and buy you a drink. They will want to relate your experiences, and to ask you about prisoners still inside and for you to help in whatever way you can. It is perfectly natural and, I feel, right for them to do so and for you to offer whatever help you can. But you have to ensure that you have your own time and space to celebrate in your own way. A quiet walk in the park, a holiday, a day of being a 'couch-potato' and doing nothing more than watching TV – in these and other small ways I celebrate my freedom every day.

In October the paperwork was completed on my flat and I was ready to move. My parents accompanied me when I picked up the keys to my new home. They were staying for a week, which passed quite quickly as we bought bed linen, crockery, pots and pans and all the other paraphernalia needed to build up a home. It was the first place I could say was truly mine and I delighted in sorting out such mundane matters as getting the electricity and the telephone connected. The world didn't seem so very different from the one I'd left nearly nineteen years earlier. I had seen it through a television screen and was aware of the many problems involved in buying and running a flat. Through my work with computers I knew of the technological advances, the microwaves and cash dispensers. Their existence is only one of the far from trivial problems for some newly released inmates. My impression of trivialities is created by the conversations of those around me: the tap's leaking again, the bus is late, the weather's terrible. I find myself unable to show concern or even involve myself in such prattle. Life is too important to me now; I feel I cannot waste time in idle conversation.

I seldom see my neighbours, though I sometimes hear them or smell their cooking, so I do have a sense of solitude here. I like this. Far from it worrying me, I really appreciate being able to decide when I'm going to be sociable and have lots of friends round and when I want to be by myself. I am fortunate enough to have many friends on whom I can call if I ever get a twinge of loneliness. I don't cook, it's not really worth it for one person. I use the microwave mostly, experimenting with the variety of frozen meals that are abundantly available. Sometimes I go out with a few friends for a meal. I'm really not that interested in food: prison has ensured that eating large portions of nutritious and wholesome food is a habit I may never become accustomed to. I like to go shopping though, and enjoy a weekly trip to Sainsbury's to stock up the cupboards.

I thought I might have found the enormity of London daunting, yet those last years spent in the large, noisy community of Holloway prepared me to some extent. I love the movement and colour, the noise of the cars during the day and most of the night. The frenetic motion on the streets is a welcome contrast to the slower, sometimes static atmosphere of places like Durham. There was only one time when I became slightly freaked out. My parents and I had been shopping in Oxford Street and we entered a department store cafeteria for a rest and a bite to eat. The tables were placed in small booths, which were surrounded on three sides by a high lattice work frame. I don't know what really affected me. For a moment I felt nauseated by the sight of so many people shovelling down indifferent food, which appeared to be piled high on their plates. The clang, clatter and crush of the place made me feel as if I was caged into the booth and I became slightly claustrophobic. We made our exit as quickly as possible. Since then, I prefer to find somewhere less crowded and more open in design.

I looked forward to the Christmas of 1992 as much as any child. I trotted happily around Oxford Street, amongst grim-faced and teeth-gritted crowds who probably thought the smiling woman coming towards them was a bit of a loony. My parents came down with my sister and her son; it was a tight squeeze at night, but the ever useful sofabeds ensured we all slept well. I had bought a Christmas tree and decorations, food was crammed in the cupboards and drink under the sink. My mother wanted to cook Christmas dinner but I refused to let her, booking us into a hotel near the park instead.

Some months earlier I had bought myself a car. Having driven before, I soon found myself back into the swing of nipping in and out of the traffic, cursing and swearing as most London drivers soon learn to do. As Christmas approached, I wondered what I was going to buy my parents. This Christmas was very special to them and the presents had to reflect that. They had an old banger, which I felt wasn't safe for them to be travelling around in; it had already broken down several times, leaving them stranded on the motorway. I decided to buy them a new one. With the help of a car sales manager I had it delivered outside my block on Christmas Eve. I had parked it right under the window of the flat.

On Christmas Day, woken earlier than usual by my nephew, we exchanged our presents, I had bought my parents odd little items which they duly opened. I handed an oblong parcel to Sam. Inside was a chocolate car from Thornton's and an envelope holding the keys of the new car. On seeing the chocolate car, Sam laughed and said it would probably go better than his old banger. He then opened the envelope. He stared in confusion at the car keys for a moment. I told him to look out of the window. They were both speechless, full of emotion and disbelief. It gave me the greatest pleasure to give them that car, expensive as it was. They had spent years driving up and down the country to visit me in prison in old bangers and it was only what they deserved. Later that day we all jumped in the new car and drove down to the hotel for our Christmas dinner. It was the first real Christmas of my life.

Shortly after I was released, I went back to Holloway to visit friends. It seemed rather odd that first time. I was allowed to go into the education department and passed through corridors and rooms I had never been allowed access to when I was an inmate. It was extraordinary to be let in rather than locked in. I met my friends Anne and Lisa and was happy to see the DTP business still flourishing. It was a weird feeling to wander through the department, knowing I could leave at any time I wished. I was extremely conscious of the fact and felt slightly uncomfortable. Although I felt at ease with my friends, telling them the crack and what I had been doing since release, our relationship was now on another level and I wasn't quite sure whether I liked it or not.

There's so much about life in prison I'd like to see change and although I'd hate to find myself emblematic of a cause, a figurehead of any kind, if there are problems I can draw attention to, I will. For instance, I deplore the recent decision by the Home Office to privatise prison education. To run a prison for profit seems most mercenary to me and rules out any chance of future 'rehabilitation' for those inmates locked up. The idea of prison education being run by such companies as Group 4 security, who have already made news with the many inmates who have escaped from their care, seems ludicrous and astonishing. What kind of prison teaching experience would a security group have? For years the education staff in Holloway have provided not only a high standard of teaching but also substantial moral support to inmates, based on many years of experience. I cannot see why, if the present system works, there is any need to change it. The government's idea seems to be that competition increases quality. In a time of recession and high unemployment, over a thousand teachers in prisons all over the country will have to reapply for their jobs when the work is handed over to individual contractors. Many of the teachers have already received redundancy notices and the chances of their being reinstated by their new employers are very slight.

The medical treatment in prisons has always come under criticism and plans are under way to bring the medical department into the NHS. This is a very positive step and will, hopefully, provide a better standard of treatment for inmates. The general attitude of the medical staff in prisons is that most inmates are hypochondriacs, and probably malingerers, so most complaints aren't taken seriously. Many inmates have little or no trust in the present medical services and, more importantly, mistakes are often made by prison doctors in their diagnoses.

Since release I have been asked to attend meetings and

vigils to highlight certain issues surrounding prisons. I have joined those members who made up my support group to form a support group for other wrongfully convicted inmates, our concern at the moment being focused on the case of the East Ham two, Prem Sivalingham and Sam Kulasingham. Although I didn't want to become involved with pressure groups, it would be impossible for me not to do what I can. If there's a chance that by showing my face at demonstrations, vigils and meetings helps in any way, then I feel I have a responsibility to be there. I was rather nervous at the thought of public speaking, but having done a few talks by now I dread it less than I used to. I have learnt that it is much like preparing an essay for the OU, only talking it through rather than writing it down.

I would like to lead a 'normal life' now, whatever that is, but I don't think it's going to be possible. I want to forget about the whole prison issue, but I can't. I'm deeply fond of my friends and the very things we talk about and do together precludes any chance of slipping away to an anonymous life elsewhere. I have other hopes and plans, yet even these are often related to the experiences of the last eighteen years. How could they not be?

I enjoy writing and want to write for a living, plays mainly. My friend Sylvie and I have begun to work together, drawing on our experiences in the hope of producing a drama series concerning life in prison. I would like it to convey every aspect of life in a women's prison: the shame, the anger, the violence, the humour and the optimism, all of which exist. I know lots of friends who work in the writing and theatre fields and I don't kid myself. I know it is a harsh world, but I feel comfortable there. There is a little pocket of opportunities awaiting me there and, more importantly, rare new friendships that are not totally linked with the misery of the past. It must be said that I find it difficult to socialise with others. In the main I mix with people who are in some way connected either directly with my case, or with others who are involved with civil liberties, pressure groups and inmates' organisations. I don't feel the need to explain myself with them, they know me and my background. I sometimes dread the friendly encounters with people outside this world. After the, 'Where do you come from?' and 'What do you do?' comes the moment when I have to explain, and I'm tired of explaining. There wouldn't be any point – even if I was tempted – in saying 'Oh, I worked at boring jobs in the north of England for years', even though this is true in a way, because most people eventually twig who I am and then come the same old questions: what was it like, are you bitter, what are you doing now? It doesn't really bother me that much, but it certainly limits my social life.

Another odd aspect of prison is the way that many people often stay almost the same age as when they came in. It sometimes makes social adjustment difficult: although one matures over the years, there is always a little part of you that reacts as if you're twenty-four instead of forty-four. I think it's to do with the fact that you're not really living whilst in prison, you're waiting – frozen, embalmed, enduring. Birthdays don't mean much beyond the fact that it's an excuse to buy yourself some treat and have an apology of a party with your friends. In some ways the clock stops. If you don't see people regularly, you forget that they, too, are growing and expect your baby brother to be the kid he was in a photograph, not the tall, well-built bloke with the moustache that he is. You're locked in some kind of time-warp that makes it hard to adapt to family and friends you had before. Not that I was unaware of time passing: I kept diaries and marked off the days like a latterday version of those cartoons of old men in prison chalking their days up on the cell wall with their manacle-free hand. In all, I chalked up some 6,696 days, give or take a leap year!

Of course there is always the 'No smoke' brigade, those people with an unshakeable faith in British justice who hold a range of racial, social and political prejudices. They believe that no one who gets into the sort of trouble I did can be entirely innocent. If I, or anyone else convicted of an IRA-related offence (indeed, this is even applied to those who have been released on appeal), hadn't actually been involved this time, well, there were bound to be previous atrocities for which they had not been caught. I don't allow these people to bother me, my feelings towards them lie somewhere between pity and contempt; they are ignorant, blinkered people.

At home I often sit in the twilight, adapting to the gloom and not noticing that it's dusk outside until I find I can't read any more or perhaps a visitor will suggest that we switch a light on. I feel this is a kind of celebration, a reaction to the years of harsh overhead fluorescents, control over which was held by the officers. There are many small ways in which my feelings about being free are expressed every day. Yet not an hour goes by when I don't think of prison. The following short piece I wrote many years ago in Durham sums up my thoughts and feelings correctly.

When you get out, you'll put prison behind you like a bad dream – someone once said to me.

How can I forget? Every nuance of this place is known to me. Every echo of a closing door. Every sliding, shuffling footstep. Every voice unseen I recognise. I know what is happening before it happens, every minute of every day and what will happen in future days.

Even in the silence of the night, footsteps tiptoe in my mind, keys jingle, spyholes squeak, a soft sobbing disturbs my sleep, a faint humming of some lonely soul's radio. On the wind is carried a faint trembling rattle of a train.

All of these things and more of which I am unconsciously aware, invade my dreams, become part of me – my nightmare, I can never put them behind me.

They are embedded in my soul, they will, in turn, become part of my memories – never forgotten – called upon endlessly, without thought.

If, once free, through some aberration of the mind, I chance to forget. I look around, at my parents aged and withered, at the children grown without me – at the world turning – at the wasted life that is me.

Never could I forget, put it all behind me. I will never forget – more importantly – I will never let you forget.

Index

AIDS, prisoners suffering
from 123-4
Aldershot 26
An Phoblacht 27
Andrea 137
Angela 61
Anne 141-2, 153, 173
Anne Yvonne 24, 50
appeal system 59

Baader-Meinhof group 41
backslang 73
Baker, Kenneth 150
Battle of Bogside 23
Bax, Bunty 147
Belfast 23
BelleVue 31
Birmingham six 112, 132,
139, 143, 148, 149, 150,
164, 170
Blake, Nick 151, 152, 162
Bowden, Dr 161
Brady, Ian 42
Brecht, Bertolt
The Caucasian Chalk Circle
142
Bridget 20
Buffini, Fiona 142
Buffini, Moira 142
Bywaters, Edith 144-5

Camden Town 18
Cardiff 33
Carol (co-employee of Ward
in Wiltshire) 16-17
Carol (teacher, Holloway)
137
Caroline 78, 81-3
Carrie 137
Cartwright, Jim
To 142
Category A prisoners 45,
47-8, 60, 62, 67, 89-90,
106-7
Catterick 25
Chipperfield's circus 31-2
Chipping Norton 32
Chippy (Mr Chips) 113, 116,
121
civil rights marches 22
Clarke, Sister Sarah 114
Cohn Bendit, Daniel 41
Colin 124, 128, 137
Conlon, Gerry 58
Conlon, Giuseppe 58
Cookham Wood Prison
107-8, 114-30, 137
Corbyn, Jeremy 147
cutting up 2-3

Dan 27
Deathwatch 60

Debbie 119, 128
Delia 137
Derry 23
Devlin, Bernadette 23
Dewsbury Magistrate's
 Court 34-5
Dublin 27
Dundalk 19, 21
Durham Prison 1-4, 41-116,
 130-4, 177

East Ham two 175
Eddie 137
 Shambles Corner 137
Elaine 28-31
Ellis, Ruth 145
Entebbe attack 41
Euston station bomb 29-31
 Ward charged with 34
Eva 110-11
Eve 114
Ewan 137

Farrell, Michael 114, 159
France 169-70

Germaine, Lisa 16
Germaine, Mrs 16-17
Gillespie sisters 59, 131
Glidewell, Lord Justice
 159-61, 163, 166
Gould, Julie 147
Gould, Peter 147
Great Train Robbers 42
Gudjonsson, Dr 149, 157, 161
Guevara, Che 22-3
Guildford 25
Guildford four 18, 58, 112,
 131-2, 148, 149, 151

Guildford pub bombings 39,
 59

Hadaway, Tom 113-14
 Yesterday's Children 114
Helen 2-3
Henderson, Paul 167
Hess, Rudolf 68
Higgs, Mr 162
Hilary 137
HIV positive prisoners 123
Hodgkinson, Peter 60
Holloway Prison 129-30,
 135-62, 173-4
Home Office, appeals to 68

Ian 154
Ireland 18-24, 21
 Northern *see* Northern
 Ireland
 Ward's political views 9,
 21-2
Iris 158
Irish Republican Army
 (IRA) 18, 41
 Provisional IRA 23
Isle of Man 19
Italy, student protests 23

Jac 137
Jack 28
Jackie 101-2
Jane 103
Janet 2-3
John 23-4
Julie 31
June 2

Keady 21
Kelly, Nicky 170

Khloud 77-8, 81-3
King, Martin Luther 23
Kitty 20
Koestler, Arthur 110
Kray twins 42
Kropotkin, Prince Peter 156
Kulasingham, Sam 175

Langdale, Mr 159-60, 161,
    163
Latimer College bomb attack
    Ward charged with 34
lesbian relationships in
    prisons 78-9
Linda 133-4
Lisa 82, 141, 153, 173
Liverpool 5-9, 33
Logan, Alastair 112-13,
    149-50
London 28, 32-3
    IRA bombing campaigns
    18, 28-9, 59
Longford, Lord 71
Lorna 73, 79, 81-3, 120, 122,
    124-5, 126, 129
Lymme Park 13-14

M62 bombing
    Ward charged with 34
MacKeith, Dr 149, 157, 159,
    160, 161
Maguire, Anne 58-9, 60,
    103-4, 112, 131, 159
Maguire seven 58, 112, 148,
    162
Mansfield, Michael 151, 152,
    159, 162
Maria 102-3
Marie 123-4
Mary (friend in Dublin) 27

Mary (prisoner in Durham
    Prison) 103
Mary (prisoner in Durham
    Prison) 3
Matrix Churchill case 167
Maureen (employee at
    Peirce's office) 165
Maureen (prisoner) 86
May, Paul 143, 158, 159
Mogg, Martin 109
Monica 2-3
Mountbatten, Lord
    assassination 131
Mullin, Chris 147, 159

Nancy (niece) 88
Nolan, Lord Justice 159
Northern Ireland 21-2, 27,
    28
    British army presence 23
    civil rights marches 22-3
    Republican clubs banned
    23

O'Conlon, Anne 19-21, 23,
    27
O'Conlon, Bill 19, 20-1
O'Conlon, Kenneth 20-1
Olivia 153
Open University (OU) 57,
    110, 111, 124, 131

Palestine Liberation
    Organisation (PLO) 41,
    77
Paris Commune, 1968 23, 41
Peirce, Gareth 150-3, 156-7,
    160, 162-6, 168
Personal Officer Scheme 76
Peter 118-19

Polly 24
Porridge 100
Power, Billy 139, 143, 158, 159, 164, 170-1
Price sisters 29
prison argot 73-4
Prison Officers' Association (POA) 127
prison officers and staff 65, 75-6, 79, 84-7, 93
prison regime
  adjudication 69-71
  aggro bell 46, 104
  appeals to Home Office 68
  applications 50
  association time 2, 45, 63-4, 120-1
  bang-up 65
  Category A prisoners 45, 47-8, 60, 62, 67, 89-90, 106-7
  Christmas 93-7
  clothing 51
  drugs 104-5
  Durham Prison, H Wing 42-5
  educational facilities 57-8, 92-3, 110, 123-4, 137, 141-2, 174
  enforced solitude 53
  exercise 98-9, 106
  food 80-2, 83, 118
  freeflow 136
  grasses 85
  hygiene and personal appearance 43, 46, 53, 71-2, 82
  institutionalisation 46, 63
  Labour classes 118

lesbian activities 79
male prisoners, contact with 79-80
mentally disturbed inmates 101-2
mother and baby units 143-6
nonces 125-6
officers and staff 116
parole 98
Personal Officer Scheme 76
prison visitors 69-70, 70-1
private spends 52, 69, 112
privileges, systems of 120
probation service 48-9, 60
property check 35-6
punishment 69-71
red band 138, 140-1
rehabilitation 155-6, 174
remand (house arrest) 69
Rule 43 36-7
sanitation 132
self-mutilation 53, 145
slopping out 46, 82, 83
strip cell 101
strip-search 65-7
suicide attempts 2-3, 42, 53, 103
television 99-100
violence 100-4
visitors and correspondents, regulations as to 47-8, 62, 87-8, 112, 146-7
Ward's strategy to cope with 63-5
work and wages 51-2, 57, 69, 109, 118, 122-3, 124-5, 137-9

Prisoner, Cell Block H 100
probation service 60

Ravensdale 19-24, 22, 27
Richard 137, 138, 141
Risley Remand Centre 35-8,
41
Robinson, Carole 58-9, 131
Royal Ulster Constabulary
(RUC) 21, 23, 27

Sam (stepfather) 22, 61, 112,
146, 164, 166, 170, 171-3
Semley 16-17
Shaftesbury 16
Sheila 88
Sinn Fein 28-9
Sivalingham, Prem 175
Skuse, Dr 35, 132, 148
Steyn, Lord Justice 159
Stockport 10-15, 31
Styal Prison 78, 107-8, 143,
145
support groups
generally 143, 175
Ward's 113, 142-3, 147-8,
158, 159, 164, 165
Susan 94-6
Sylvie 121, 124, 129, 170, 175

Terry 137
Thompson, Emma 151-2
Thompson, Mr 166
Tummin, Judge 130

Vietnam War 22-3

Wakefield Crown Court
39-41
Ward, Anne (sister) 10

Ward, Elaine (sister) 10
Ward, Eric (brother) 10,
169-70
Ward, Ethel (mother) 10-12,
37, 50, 61-2, 112, 146,
164, 166, 170, 171-3
second marriage 22
Ward, Judith
appeal 143, 149-67
appendectomy 37-8
army 25-6, 28
arrest, 1974 5-9, 33
braille, work in 111
Category A
decategorisation 106-7
childhood and family
10-14, 61-2
children's home, taken to
11-12
compensation payment
169
confession 7-9
education 12-13
educational achievements
in prison 57, 110-11, 124,
131
employment 15-17, 19
forensic evidence against
7, 30-1, 34-5, 161, 162,
163, 166
foster home 12
horse management exams
17
hunger strike 81-3, 97
hysterectomy 88-91, 144
Koestler award 110
linked to gun discovered
at Cookham Wood
126-9
marriage proposal 23-4

police questioning 6-9, 29-31
prison medical reports 40
prison sentence 41
prison staff's attitude towards 97, 123, 126-9
release from prison 163-4
suicide attempts 1-4, 38, 160
support group 113, 142-3, 147-8, 158, 159, 164, 165
trial 39-41

undisclosed police evidence 40
weight loss 46-7
Ward, Peter (brother) 10
Ward, Terence (brother) 10
Ward, Terence (father) 10-11
Within these Walls 100
Women in Prison 82
women prisoners, treatment of, generally 91-2
Wright, Joan 125-6